I0683436

Wired 4 Connection

Wired 4 Connection

Transform your Horse Training with the Polyvagal Principles

A Guide to Understanding the Nervous System
for True Connection and Optimal Learning

Lucie Klaassen

Illustrations by Rozenn Grosjean
Cover image by Anne Mette Graumann
Author image by Susan Wijs

For more information, email info@lucieklaassen.com

ISBN: 979-8-89316-921-8 - Paperback
ISBN: 979-8-89316-920-1 - Ebook

GET FREE ADDITIONAL RESOURCES

To get the most out of this book, I have created some supplements that will help you implement the polyvagal principles in your horse training. They include:

1) A short video of my horse Jajão going through the different states of the nervous system. From a book it may be hard to recognize the states in your horse, so in this video you will *see* what the states look like. Great for visual learners.

2) A short video of me with Jajão while "giving a break" and practicing self-regulation. This video went viral on Instagram and received more than one million views within two weeks.

3) Video tutorials of the top three self-regulating strategies (from Part III of this book) that will help you move from fearful and frustrated to calm and connected.

4) A pre-training plan to set you and your horse up for an optimal training session.

GET FREE ADDITIONAL RESOURCES

Get access here:

https://rebrand.ly/W4Cbook

I dedicate this book to everyone who loves horses
and to all horses that deserve to be loved

*specifically to my horse Jajão, who taught
me the real meaning of patience*

CONTENTS

Appendices

FOREWORD

Lucie Klaassen has what we would wish all horse owners to have: patience, intuition, a passion for understanding and connecting with the horse, and a willingness to continue to learn.

Lucie has all of these in droves, but what makes her—and this book—special is her ability to take something as scientific and complex as polyvagal theory and the autonomic nervous system, and translate it into something that we as horse people can understand and relate to on the level of our own experience.

I'm not a science person. Most of what I've learned about the horse has come through observing. Even using terms like "sympathetic," "parasympathetic," and "autonomic nervous system" makes me, well...nervous. Lucie has used her experience and insight to translate the complex world of neuroscience into a relatable and practical tool that will help you truly understand how your horse learns, connects with you, and sees the world. From riding to groundwork to partnership, this book creates an inner bridge between your and your horse's experience of the world.

Lucie says she believes that certain horses come into your life for a reason. Certain learning also comes into our lives for a reason. There may be a reason you're holding this book in your hands at this point in time. Just sayin'...

Jim Masterson
Author of *The Masterson Method – Beyond Horse Massage*

INTRODUCTION

It is with joy and gratitude that I write this introduction page. I am grateful you have picked up this book to join me in the fascinating world of Polyvagal Theory. I'm also grateful for the journey of life, allowing me to see the gifts every challenge has offered me. I'm grateful for the horses that have crossed my path. Each and every one of them has taught me a different aspect of life, whether physical, mental, emotional or spiritual.

Horses have been my "lifesavers" many times, so I want to give back to horses, and I can only do this through you. You are holding this book in your hands, so I know you love horses, and that you want to be the best human you can be for them.

Horses don't care what you do; they care how you make them feel. They want to be with you when they feel **safe** with you. Feeling safe is the key element in Polyvagal Theory, and we will explore together how we can integrate the polyvagal principles into your horse training, entering a universal world of connection.

If you want to gain a deeper understanding of the connection between the brain, the functions of the autonomic nervous system (ANS), and effective training, then this is for you. Understanding the ANS will help you work better with your horse's true nature. You can even help your horse release stored tension and trauma in the body.

I strongly believe every training, no matter what discipline, consists of two parts. The first and most important part is trust, connection and communication. This is what we will explore in this book. Only after establishing a foundation of connection and understanding should you begin the physical aspect of the training. This will be covered in my next book.

In Part I, I will give you *simple* explanations about neuroscience. I will not be delving into the scientific background of hormones and neurotransmitters released by the brain. I want to keep it practical and simple, so it will benefit you and your horse, increasing understanding and welfare. Part II will be about translating the polyvagal principles to horse training. In Parts III and IV, I will give you practical tips and exercises you can apply in a range of everyday training scenarios. I sometimes repeat a certain subject from a different perspective because I know how the brain works. Repetition will help you remember.

I have been teaching groundwork and riding lessons for many years. I have held clinics all over the world and created several online courses related to horse training. However, no matter the country, age or background of the participants, the key questions and desires are always the same: "How do I achieve true connection with my horse? I want my horse to *want* to be with me. I want to have fun and be confident again like when I was younger."

I see so much frustration in the horse world, often due to a lack of connection and/or miscommunication. Horse owners come to me because of the "problems" they have in their horse training. However, I have learned it's often not the horse, it's the human who needs to be "trained." More specifically, it's the nervous system that needs to learn to regulate itself again. People want to connect with their horse but they are not connected with themselves.

If you recognize any of this, I warmly welcome you to join me on this journey of the ANS. I believe that learning about Polyvagal Theory and how you can apply it to horses will help you bring more joy and ease in anything you do with your horse.

Incorporating the polyvagal principles into your horse training is a change in lifestyle that will help both *you* and your horse. In this book I will show how you can develop easy habits and practices to stay present, calm and connected, and create a positive learning environment.

You will learn how to become a **nervous system navigator** so you don't spook when your horse spooks, you laugh instead of getting frustrated when your horse doesn't give you the response you want, you don't worry about what other people think and you can go for a relaxed trail ride.

I wish with all my heart that understanding Polyvagal Theory and applying the principles in your horse training will help you and your horse as much as it's helped me and mine.

Note: When I talk about horses, I refer to them with the pronouns he/him, but if you have a mare you can read this as she/her.

WHY LISTEN TO ME?

Allow me to start with my personal story.

A few years ago, I realized that for most of my adulthood I had been in a state of constant alertness and was experiencing "high achievement stress." My body gave me several warning signs; however, at that time I didn't know how to listen. So my body gave me a stronger warning by just collapsing. I found myself falling from being a high-achieving person into a deep depression. I was even hospitalized. This took me on a journey of unveiling the trauma stuck in my body and learning how to release the stored stress.

I share this because there is a relationship between trauma stuck in the body and horse riding. With trauma, I don't mean just big impact trauma like an accident or abuse. Trauma is any event where the nervous system has been overwhelmed, either a short impactful event or for a longer time, causing it to go into survival mode. Your nervous system, which is your safety and coping mechanism, does this when it cannot deal with the situation, storing the effects of the event in your body.

What was my trauma? My mother was diagnosed with bipolar disorder. When I was a child I never knew whether she was going to be up or down. During my childhood, she was hospitalized many times, ranging from a few weeks to several months. Only when I learned about Polyvagal Theory a few years ago did I realize that, because of this, my nervous system had been wired for "not feeling safe" and constant alertness.

I learned as a young child to be strong and independent. My coping mechanism was to go into my head and disconnect from my feeling body. Learning was easy for me, so this resulted in being an "A" student. At school I was known as exemplary; I was never any trouble, always did my homework, and never asked for help. I graduated cum laude, which got me pretty far in life.

I didn't have my own pony as a child, but I always had ponies in my life to look after. When I look back, I realize now that this is when and how I learned to communicate with horses in a very natural way. I spent all my free time with those ponies because they were my safe place. There was no riding school and no money for a saddle, so when I wanted to ride, I had to "explain" to the pony to come to the fence so I could hop on.

Fast forward to adulthood. My logical mind enabled me to fit into the corporate scene and I had a successful career as a business controller in various well-paid management jobs. I worked internationally in the Philippines, the Dutch Antilles and Venezuela until I had my first breakdown. I was in my early forties when I noticed the first signs I wasn't living my life's purpose (as a child I wanted to be a vet).

Ten years later, in 2019, I had my second breakdown. I didn't feel safe, I was alert and stressed all the time, and I didn't sleep anymore. I was hospitalized and I almost gave up on horses.

A year later, in 2020, my brother decided to end his life. He had been battling depression his whole life. He had the same childhood as I had, so I started to dive deeply into the effects of trauma. I had therapy that would "talk" to my body and nervous system, and not only to my cognitive brain. I learned about Polyvagal Theory and the Window of Tolerance.

I gained insight into my own childhood experiences and found a way to reconnect to my body wisdom. I was able to open my heart and ask for help. I became "the observer" of my triggers and the effect it had on my nervous system, without identifying myself with it. I learned from the books, courses and/or live events of Stephen Porges, Deb Dana, Gabor Maté, Peter Levine, Bruce Lipton (epigenetics), and Daniel Siegel (Window of Tolerance). I also studied with Dr. Stephen Peters and Sarah Schlote, learning about trauma-informed horse training (which you can learn more about at equuscience.com).

One day in 2021, I received a phone call from a friend. She told me about this horse she had. He had been born and bred in Portugal, trained for bullfighting. The scars on his body told his story. She was looking for a good home where someone would take the time to gain his trust. She knew I love doing groundwork and she pictured us together. I wasn't really looking for another horse; however, we instantly connected when I first saw him, because I recognized his constant alertness. So I bought Jajão.

I believe certain horses come into your life for a reason. I started to translate everything I had learned about trauma to help him regain trust in humans. Jajão has given me so many lessons and insights about how to deal with trauma in horses. That's what this book is about, the journey from trauma to trust.

I'm not a therapist; however, I call myself a specialist in trauma and resilience by experience. As a horse trainer and awareness & mindset coach, it is my passion to empower you and every horse owner to understand how the autonomic nervous system works, so you can reconnect with your body wisdom and become more resilient.

Learn to work *with* instead of against your ANS so you can improve the quality of connection with your horse. Bring more ease and joy into your relationship with your horse.

Become a **nervous system navigator.** Happy owner, happy horse!

PART I

Polyvagal Theory Explained

In this part, we will dive into the fascinating world of Polyvagal Theory, a concept that forms the foundation of the polyvagal approach to horse training. Understanding Polyvagal Theory will equip you with invaluable insights into the autonomic nervous system and its role in shaping your interactions with horses.

CHAPTER 1

Understanding the Nervous System

Let us first get a global understanding of the nervous system, which is your body's command center. It has two main parts:

1. The central nervous system (CNS)

The CNS is composed of the brain and spinal cord, and serves as the main control center for your body. It interprets incoming signals, formulates responses, and plays a crucial role in higher-order functions like consciousness, memory and cognition.

2. The peripheral nervous system (PNS)

The PNS is made up of a network of nerves that branch out from the spinal cord and run through your whole body. The key role of the PNS is sending information from different areas of your body to your brain, and carrying out commands from your brain to various parts of your body and limbs, including your organs, skin and glands.

Your nervous system uses nerve cells to send electrical signals from all the parts of your body to your brain (known as interoception), and it also keeps track of what's going on outside of your body (exteroception). After processing the information, it responds to any situation you're in. Your nervous system also uses chemical compounds produced by various glands as signals for communication.

Your nerves consist of bundles of nerve cells (neurons), which have long extensions called axons. The nerve cells and their axons intertwine and form nerve fibers. There are two different types of neurons, and each has a different job:

1. Sensory neurons

Sensory neurons carry information from your senses (what you see, hear, taste, smell and touch) to your brain. They either connect directly to your brain through your cranial nerves or carry information to your spinal nerves, which then feed into your spinal cord.

2. Motor neurons

Motor neurons carry command signals from your brain to various parts of your body, like for muscle movement. They only carry information away from your brain.

Some of these electrical signals are sent with your conscious intention, while other signals are sent without you even thinking about it. That's why the peripheral nervous system is divided into two parts:

1. Somatic nervous system (SNS)

The SNS guides your voluntary movements. Your body's muscles receive signals from the brain that give them instructions on how to move around. Your somatic nervous system spreads outward from the brain through your neck in twelve pairs of cranial nerves (referred to in medicine using Roman numerals), eleven of which are part of your somatic nervous system. Cranial nerve II, for example, connects to your eyes, because your retina and optic nerve connect directly to your brain.

2. Autonomic nervous system (ANS)

The ANS regulates activities you do without thinking about them, like unconscious processes and involuntary movements. It's like the "behind the scenes" computer running the processes that keep you alive, like beating your heart, digesting food, sweating and blinking. Your ANS is always active, even when you're asleep, and it's key to your continued survival.

Some bodily activities can be controlled by the ANS as well as the SNS, like breathing. Under most circumstances, you breathe automatically and without thinking about it. But you can also breathe consciously, deliberately controlling when and how long you inhale and exhale.

The traditional view of the ANS is that it consists of two parts:

1. Sympathetic nervous system (SNS)

The SNS is responsible for all processes that activate the body. When danger or stress arises, it also activates the body's stress response so the body can prepare for an active defense against the perceived threat by running away or by opposing the threat (known as the fight-or-flight response).

2. Parasympathetic nervous system (PNS)

The PNS is the SNS's counterpart, and takes care of returning to normal functioning of many systems, undoing the stress response, and generating a state of calm and ease, once the stressful event is over (known as the rest-and-digest response). This includes relaxing the muscles as well as digestion and recovery.

You can explore these two branches of your ANS yourself. Taking a deep breath activates the SNS, making you ready to sprint off. Slowly exhaling, on the other hand, stimulates the PNS and you relax. Through targeted breathing, you can influence your ANS (I will talk more about breathing and self-regulating in Part III).

The ANS is considered by many to work like a light switch; when one system is active, the other system is off. This on/off model is still widely used, also in the horse world; and while much of this information is accurate, it turns out this two-system model is outdated and too simplistic. The PNS is actually more complex than previously thought. This is at the heart of Polyvagal Theory, and we will be exploring it in detail in Chapter 5.

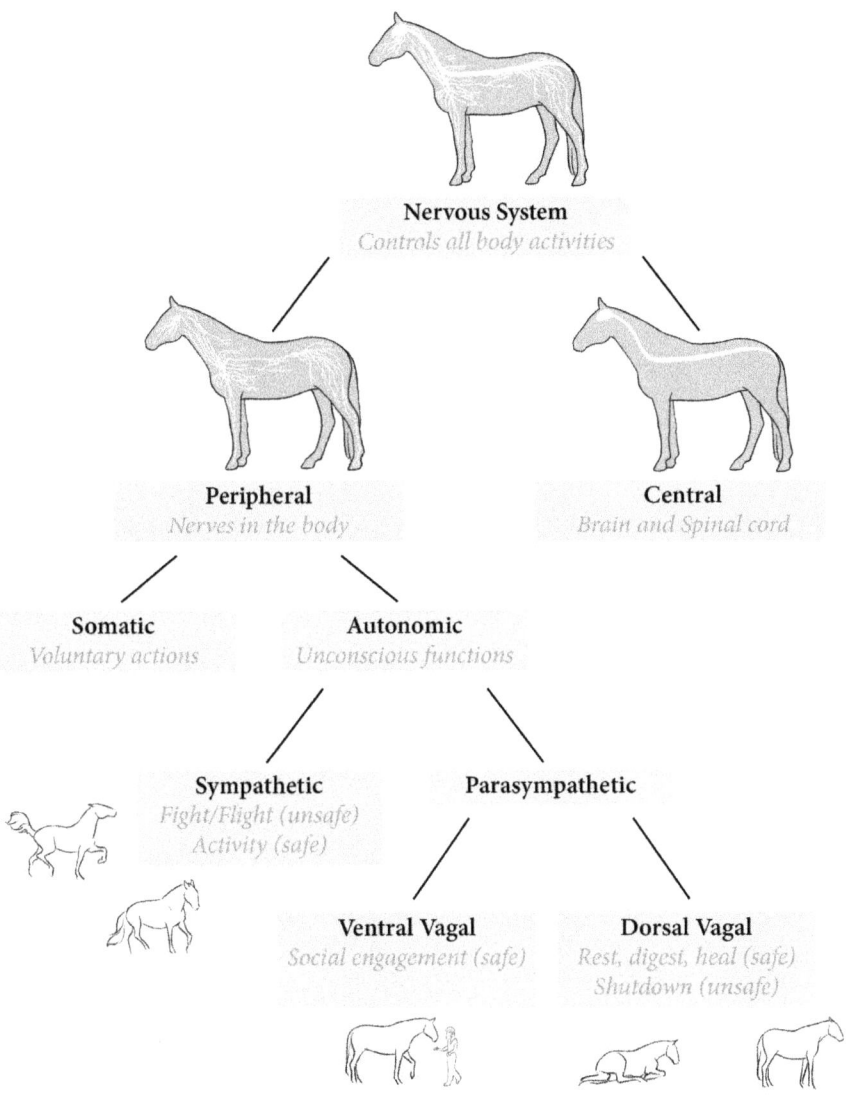

Nervous System
Controls all body activities

Peripheral
Nerves in the body

Central
Brain and Spinal cord

Somatic
Voluntary actions

Autonomic
Unconscious functions

Sympathetic
Fight/Flight (unsafe)
Activity (safe)

Parasympathetic

Ventral Vagal
Social engagement (safe)

Dorsal Vagal
Rest, digest, heal (safe)
Shutdown (unsafe)

CHAPTER 2

Early Wiring of the Nervous System

Most of the development of our brain happens in the first five years of our life. A newborn baby has all its brain cells (neurons); however, it's the *connections between these cells* that make the brain work. About 90 percent of our brain gets "wired" from birth to age five. That's more than at any other time in life.

I only recently understood *why* early wiring is so important. ***It is the foundation for our core beliefs about life and our behavior as an adult.***

In our first few years of life, we need to learn so many essential skills, like crawling, walking and talking, in a relatively short time. This is why there are so many new connections formed in the brain at such a young age.

These early brain connections set the stage for the development of our brain later in life. How our brain develops in our early years has a huge impact on our brain as an adult, including three very important life skills—our future **responses to stress**, the ability to **learn,** and our openness to **connect** with others. It's much harder for these essential brain connections to be formed later in life.

This explains why childhood experiences, especially the very earliest, are of significant importance for later development. Neurons that fire together wire together, meaning that brain connections (or neural pathways) used often grow stronger, while brain connections not used will be eliminated. This is similar to our muscles—use it or lose it.

Have a look inside my brain:

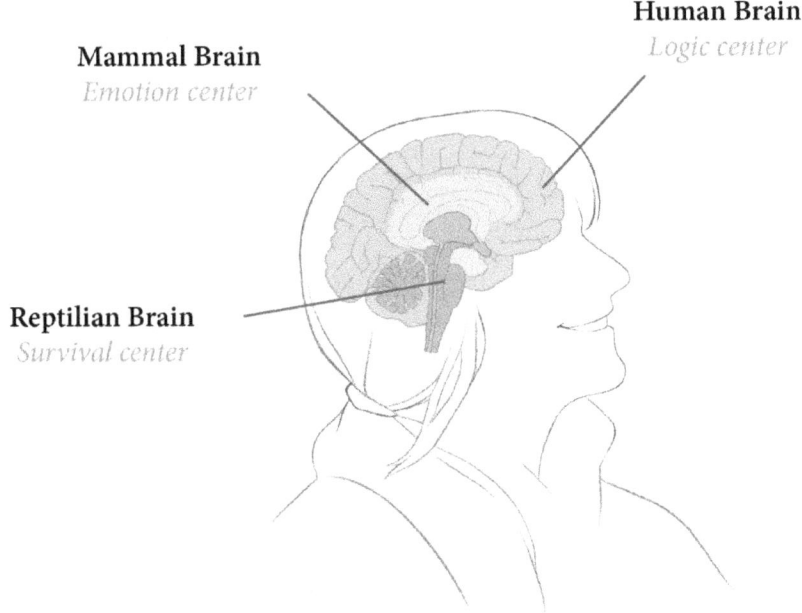

Human Brain
Logic center

Mammal Brain
Emotion center

Reptilian Brain
Survival center

The wiring in our brain develops differently depending if we feel safe or unsafe. So how does healthy brain development happen? How are these connections in the brain wired? Let me explain based on the early development of our brain and the wiring of our nervous system.

1. Reptilian brain or brainstem

The brainstem is our survival center. It is responsible for the fight, flight and freeze response. The reptilian brain is fully developed at birth. It handles basic instincts and functions to sustain life like breathing, digestion, hydration, sleep and body temperature. Starting from birth, we develop brain connections through everyday experiences. During the first year, a baby learns through his or her senses—observing faces, touching objects, listening to voices and sounds. They build connections in the brain through interacting with the world around them.

2. Mammal brain or limbic system

The limbic system is our emotional center. Its main development is between birth and five years old. The mammal brain is responsible for our emotional responses and memory. It is often referred to as the "seat of learning." It also controls how we deal with stress. Toddlers primarily use their emotional brain. Their self-expression and communication are expressed in the form of feelings and (sometimes loud) emotions.

3. Human brain or prefrontal cortex

The prefrontal cortex is the executive center, or the thinking brain, and is the last area to be developed, starting around the age of five and only fully developed in our early twenties. It is responsible for rational thinking, planning, attention, self-awareness, problem-solving, decision-making, interpretation and understanding.

Children from the age of five have an idea of what is right or wrong, have a sense of self, and can empathize. They develop cognitive understanding and have a better capacity to control impulses.

There is significant neurological growth in the temporal and frontal lobes, and these connections allow for increased ability to process emotions.

All this means that during the first five years of our life, we have *no filter*. We cannot understand what is right or wrong as we are *not yet capable of interpreting* what is happening. Everything that enters our brain from the outside world is *considered the truth*, especially when it comes from our main caregivers.

So, if you were told as a child that you are stupid, then this is what *you believe about yourself*. If you experience when you're getting high grades that you are loved, and when you get low grades you're put in a corner, your brain wires itself to believe you're only "good enough" when you deliver high performance. This is how you may become a perfectionist, for example, by thinking that being perfect is the only way you "deserve" love.

If those vital connections of feeling safe aren't strengthened through attachment, children are deprived of the experiences they need to grow the prefrontal cortex. Learning and executive functions are compromised, and children remain unable to regulate their emotions and behaviors in response to their experience of the world.

This is how you form your *core beliefs* about yourself, and your ensuing adult life is largely based on whether or not you felt safe during your early years. This is how you are conditioned in early life. This is why so many people feel unworthy or not good enough.

Let me explain it in another way. When we are born, we have two essential yet contradicting drives:

1. Belonging

I want to connect, I want to belong, I want to feel safe, I want to be held. Since we cannot survive without our parents or caregivers, this drive is our most essential one. It is a foundational survival need, as we need to be held and feel safe for co-regulation.

2. Authenticity and uniqueness

I want to be me, I want to express myself, I want to be heard, I want to be seen. From this drive, we want to explore the world and learn that we have a unique voice that wants to be expressed.

When infants start to explore the world, following the drive to express themselves, they operate from the survival center. Infants are totally dependent on their parents or major caregivers. They are unable to regulate their own system, so they totally rely on a connected caregiver to soothe them and cope with any situation they encounter. Through a positive, stable, nurturing relationship with their major caregivers, they learn to feel safe as a child.

From this secure space they explore the world around them, knowing they can always come back to a safe haven. They can safely expand their world without fear because they know they're loved and supported. This safety includes physical well-being, as in not getting hurt, and emotional safety and regulation.

Learning how to deal with stress is also part of a healthy development. When a young child experiences stress, the stress response system is activated. There is an adrenaline rush, and the body is brought into a state of alertness, through such things as an increased heart rate and a rush of blood to the muscles. When the stress trigger disappears and the young child is comforted by the safe and soothing presence of a parent or caregiver, the body goes back into homeostasis.

Many studies show that caring interaction with parents or major caregivers in the first days, weeks, months and years of life helps the brain grow a strong and healthy network of connections. In a supportive environment, co-regulation can be learned. Co-regulation is the exchange between caregivers and children of emotions and responses, a process that provides a secure anchor for the child's developing nervous system. When children feel safe, seen and soothed by their caregivers, the neural pathways associated with safety and trust can be wired.

Parents or major caregivers become the architects of this foundational wiring. Their ability to create a safe haven for their children sets the stage for healthy self-regulation in the future. In a safe and nurturing environment, children learn that their emotions are acknowledged and validated, paving the way for the development of emotional intelligence.

Unfortunately, the other direction is also true. Neuroscience studies show the negative impact of not feeling safe and experiencing trauma in one's early years. When there is no safe haven, when caregivers are not attuned to the child's needs, or when the environment is filled with instability, the wiring takes a different path. The nervous system becomes attuned to a sense of danger, and the child learns to navigate the world with heightened vigilance. The brain develops fewer brain connections, especially those helping them with healthy attachments and connections.

As children internalize these early experiences, the wiring of their nervous system becomes a blueprint for adulthood. Those who have experienced a secure and nurturing environment are more likely to develop robust self-regulation skills. They carry a sense of safety within, allowing them to navigate life's challenges with resilience.

Conversely, for those who experienced instability or neglect in their early years, self-regulation can become very challenging. Their nervous system, wired for danger, may trigger stress responses even in non-threatening situations, leading to challenges in emotional regulation and forming healthy connections. If the nervous system believes it's not safe to rest and relax, it stays in an alert state all the time.

Learning all the above made me realize that my nervous system had been in a hyper-alert state most of my adult life. I needed to be "in control" by being smart, working hard and not showing any emotions. Being in my head kept me safe, and I had lost the connection to the wisdom of my body. When you're in this state for a long period of time, it has a huge effect on your health.

CHAPTER 3

How Trauma Affects Your Life

While this is not a book about trauma, I believe it's important to have some foundational understanding of trauma and how trauma affects the way we act, think and react, not only in our own lives but also in relation to horses. Most people think of trauma as the result of some significant event—an accident, abuse, or similar impactful event. However, trauma can also have a more subtle cause that can run even deeper. At times it's easy to miss the signs of this.

Trauma is not the event itself; it's the response of the brain and nervous system to an event or situation. This varies from person to person, depending on how the individual's brain has developed. In fact, two individuals can share the exact same experience, with one ending up with trauma and the other being completely fine in life.

Trauma is the (lasting) effect on your nervous system when an event happens that is perceived as unsafe, preventing you from going back to homeostasis. The event gets "stuck" in your body, and your nervous system becomes dysregulated. A layer of protection develops around it, because you don't want to experience this feeling again.

There are two main kinds of trauma:

1. Impact trauma or shock trauma

Impact trauma is caused by a clear single incident such as an operation, an accident, an incident of abuse, or the experience of war. It can even happen before or right after birth; for example, if the mother has depression and is not able to respond to the child's needs, and the baby is separated from the mother. The baby becomes isolated and there is no feeling of co-regulation and safety after the separation. This type of trauma is also called acute trauma, and it's the kind we usually correlate with the word—the palpable, more easily traceable type.

When we suffer impact trauma, it causes us to enter the fight, flight or freeze state, in which our brains become overwhelmed and disorganized. Meanwhile, the body shifts into survival mode, and the higher reasoning and language structures (prefrontal cortex) of the brain shut down.

As the traumatic event unfolds, adrenaline floods the body. The memory of the event is then imprinted in the amygdala, which is part of the limbic system. The amygdala is responsible for storing the emotional significance of the event, including its level of intensity.

When we go through our normal daily routines, the amygdala stores our events as a story. A story becomes a memory that can be placed in the past. When an event is perceived as highly dangerous, the amygdala records only the sensory data experienced during the event. It keeps score of the sights, sounds, touch, smells and tastes experienced while the event plays out. Differing from a normal stored memory, records from traumatic events are kept as fragments instead of a linear, chronological and rational story.

So it's easy to see how a person who has experienced trauma can get triggered later in life. For example, let's say you've been in a car accident. Upon impact, your body floods with adrenaline and you go into fight, flight or freeze mode. In the background, you hear the roar of the flames as the car next to yours explodes. Because your prefrontal cortex has shut down, your brain is disorganized, and the sensory fragment of a very loud sound is stored in your amygdala. Later in life, when you hear another very loud sound, you feel triggered, and your brain once again gets flooded. The rational part of your mind shuts down, so that the sound of fireworks, for example, can bring up the same panic and trauma response.

After the traumatic event, the brain is easily triggered by sensory input. To the disorganized brain, normal circumstances are interpreted as dangerous. A dropped pan can turn into a gunshot. A red light can turn into a flame. A hug can turn into sexual abuse. Because sensory input is misinterpreted, the brain after trauma has difficulty knowing which circumstances are normal and which are dangerous.

2. Process trauma or developmental trauma

The second type of trauma, known as process or developmental trauma, occurs behind the scenes. It's the hidden kind of trauma, the type that seeps in and accumulates over time.

If we grow up in an environment that doesn't feel safe, we're constantly alert and under stress. Eventually, this becomes the way we see the world, the way our brain develops to interpret the things around us. After a prolonged period of being in this alert mode, the system can no longer go back into the green zone of relaxation and stability. So even after the stressor is gone and the environment changes to normal, our system remains on high alert.

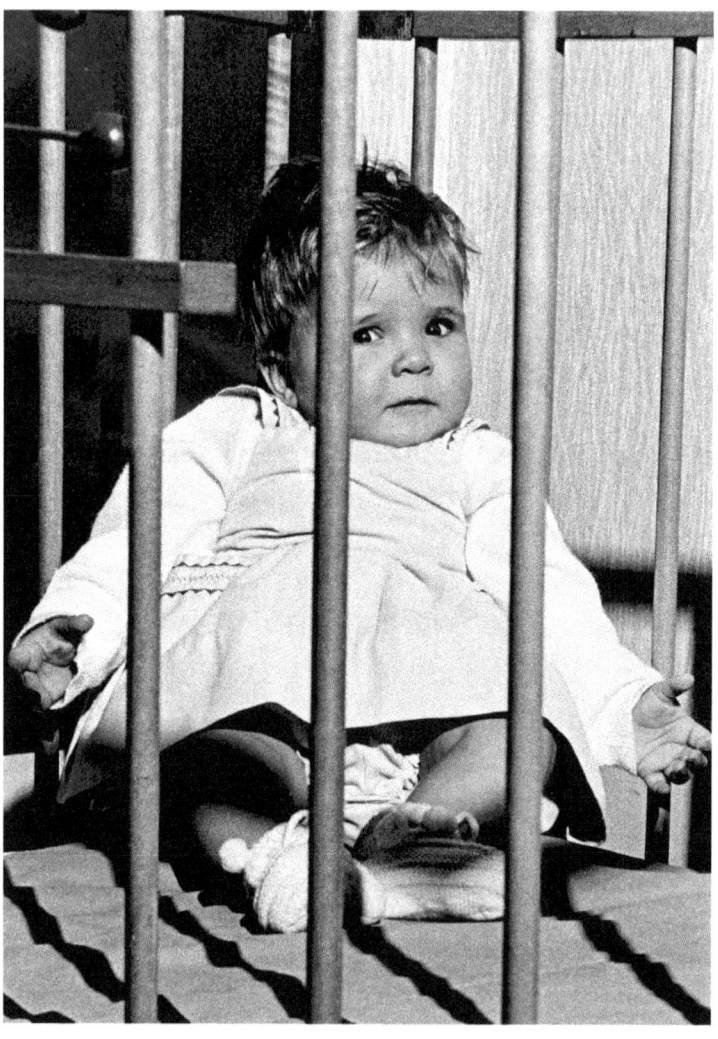

Me as a baby

The surprising truth is that almost every single one of us has undergone some kind of process trauma. We live in a broken world, and it's impossible for any of us to have had all of our needs met as we were growing up. Maybe we were bullied at school and felt it was unsafe to trust others. Or one of our parents suffered from depression or addiction and were unable to make us feel safe. Maybe there were teachers who asked too much of us, or guardians who didn't allow us to express the aspects about ourselves that make us special and different. When our needs aren't met and this happens over a prolonged period, the result is process trauma. We disconnect from our body because we don't want to feel the pain of not being safe.

A great book on understanding more about trauma is *The Body Keeps the Score* by Bessel van der Kolk. He explains how the mind, brain and body are all impacted by the effects of trauma.

Another great book is *The Myth of Normal*, by Gabor Maté. According to him, we all carry our own psychological wounds in the form of trauma. In his famous words, he says that trauma is not what happens to us, but what happens inside of us as a result of what happened to us.

The good news is that, although past events and situations can't be altered, the wounds they caused can be healed. No one is intrinsically "crazy," so we all can find ways to live life in a joyful way, free of emptiness, fear, workaholic issues, overachieving tendencies, and/or depression.

Understanding the foundational principles of how trauma will tense our body, shallow our breathing, influence our posture and more explains how trauma stuck in our body will also influence the way we deal with horses. We squeeze our legs more strongly because we want to be in control. We have tension in our shoulders and fingers from holding onto the reins. We jump up when our horse is startled by something instead of being a steady, safe human for our horse.

This is why it's important to become aware of the stored tension in your body, so that you can find ways to release it and become a steadier and safer partner for your horse.

CHAPTER 4

The Three Brains

Before we dive into the intriguing world of Polyvagal Theory, let us first take a closer look at our brains. We'll discover how different parts of our brains work in harmony with our autonomic nervous system. We touched upon the brain's development stages in Chapter 2, so now let us go deeper into the different roles of the three main parts of the brain.

Reptilian brain or brainstem: The Guardian of Basics

Imagine your brain as a house with several floors. Right at the ground level, you'll find the reptilian brain, also known as the brainstem. Think of it as a diligent caretaker, always on duty, making sure you're okay. This part of the brain handles your life-saving basics—keeping your heart beating and your lungs breathing, and making sure you're alert.

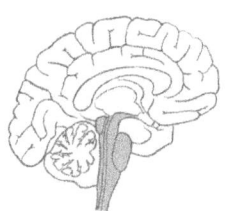

Reptilian Brain
Survival center

The reptilian brain is all about instinct. It operates on *survival and reproduction instincts,* much like a reptile that doesn't think twice before snapping at a fly. It's this part of your brain that kicks into gear when you need to react quickly to danger, like a horse's instinct to flee from threats.

Picture this: you're strolling down a peaceful street, when suddenly you hear a loud bang. Before even processing what's happening, you move yourself out of harm's way. That instant reaction is your reptilian brain in action. It sensed danger and launched you into fight-or-flight mode. If there's a perceived threat, the amygdala—your reptilian brain's key component— pumps out adrenaline and cortisol, priming your muscles and heart for quick action.

Our cave-dwelling ancestors relied heavily on this brain part for survival, constantly on the lookout for danger. Though modern life is generally safer, our amygdala still treats any *perceived* threat with the same urgency.

Sometimes our reptilian brain may seem too eager to protect us, reacting strongly to threats that aren't as dangerous as they seem. Remember, it's just doing its job to keep you safe, ensuring you're ready to act swiftly when needed.

Mammal brain or limbic system: The Seat of Emotions

The second level of our "brain house" is the limbic system. Think of the reptilian brain as the foundation, and right above it rests the mammal brain. It doesn't replace the reptilian brain; instead it enriches it, by adding layers of emotions and social interactions to our basic instincts. Imagine it as an expert translator, turning simple survival signals into complex feelings and behaviors.

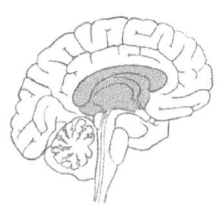

Mammal Brain
Emotion center

Just like horses and other mammals often stick together in groups for better survival, our limbic system nudges us towards forming connections and relationships. It seeks security and a sense of belonging, like how a horse feels more at ease within its herd. This part of our brain colors our experiences with a wide range of feelings. And it's specially equipped to understand others' emotions too, playing a vital role in building connections.

Inside the limbic system, there are two important parts called the hippocampus and hypothalamus. Think of them as the brain's librarians. They guide you through life, drawing on past experiences and learned behaviors. These areas are crucial for learning and memory storage.

Our emotions and feelings play a critical role in our decision-making processes, all managed by this subconscious part of our brain. The limbic system receives input from our senses via the sensory nerves, processing information before it reaches our conscious awareness. This is the basis for our "gut feelings," the intuitive insights guided by these sensory nerves.

Human brain or prefrontal cortex: The Wise Decision-Maker

The highest level of our "brain house" is the thinking brain, also known as the prefrontal cortex. This is the top part and functions as the executive control center responsible for speaking, thinking logically, understanding social cues, making plans, decision-making, and self-awareness.

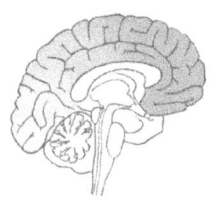

Human Brain
Logic center

We humans have a very advanced prefrontal cortex compared to animals. It acts like the overall general manager, helping us deal with complicated situations and make smart decisions. When things get tough, this part of the brain consciously decides to stay calm and can therefore make better choices.

Have you ever been really upset? Your reptilian brain might get you ready to run away or fight, and your mammal brain makes you feel all those strong emotions. But when you know how to remain calm, you're able to access your prefrontal cortex. There are ways to calm down, like taking deep breaths or talking about what you're feeling, so you can feel better. We will talk about creating new pathways to get easier access to this part of the brain in Part III of this book.

Our prefrontal cortex is also great at imagining things. It doesn't know the difference between doing something and just thinking about it. So, when we keep imagining ourselves doing well, like giving a great talk or confidently going on a relaxed trail ride, we actually become better at those things in real life.

To summarize, our amazing brains are like an orchestra; the reptilian brain starts the beat, the mammal brain adds the instruments, and the human brain is the conductor who keeps it all in beautiful harmony. When all three work together, both we and our horses feel safe, connected, and ready to create amazing partnerships.

CHAPTER 5

Polyvagal Theory

In the previous chapters, we looked at the layers and development stages of the brain. In this chapter, we take a closer look at recent discoveries about the nervous system. We will explore the essence of Polyvagal Theory, introduced by Dr. Stephen Porges in the early 1990s. This theory revolutionizes our understanding of how the nervous system responds to stress and social engagement. It explains the *science of connection and learning.*

Dr. Porges conducted groundbreaking research on the autonomic nervous system in mammals. He found that the vagus nerve, which is the main activator of the parasympathetic nervous system, has *two distinct branches* named for where they attach to the brain—the ventral (front) vagal parasympathetic branch and the dorsal (back) vagal parasympathetic branch. They run from the brainstem through the neck and chest and down to the internal organs. Because of this multiple branching, it is now called the "**Polyvagal Theory.**"

So, Polyvagal Theory asserts that you really have three systems that make up the ANS—the dorsal vagal parasympathetic nervous system, the ventral vagal parasympathetic nervous system, and the sympathetic nervous system—all working together in a coordinated way. Polyvagal Theory explains the relationship between the ANS and social behavior, and how we move through a continuous cycle of the three states every day of our lives.

Dr. Porges also introduced us to the concept of "**neuroception**." It's like a sixth sense helping us (and horses) unconsciously detect safety or danger in our environment. We will delve more into this in the next chapter; but for now, it's enough to understand that neuroception will define if we are in what's called the green, yellow or red zone.

The dorsal vagal system:
The Red Zone Emergency Brake

The dorsal vagal system is the oldest part of the nervous system. It's responsible for the "take a break" mode, also called our "rest and digest" state, when our ANS is regulated and we feel safe. However, it can also serve as our emergency system and can shut our bodies down. It's our body's way of saying, "If I play dead, it might save me," like prey caught by a lion. Here's what happens in such a shutdown mode:

- Everything goes quiet and still
- Our heart rate, breathing and metabolism all slow down
- Blood flow focuses on our core, conserving energy

In extreme situations, like during an accident or during depression, the dorsal vagal system helps us by going into a "conservation" mode.

The sympathetic system:
The Yellow Zone Ready for Action

The sympathetic system is responsible for our body's "get ready" mode. When we need to spring into action, the sympathetic part of our nervous system kicks in. When the sympathetic system is activated, it makes us ready for action, preparing us to fight or flee from danger. Here's what happens:

- Our adrenal glands get busy, sending adrenaline into our blood
- Our heart and breathing rates pick up the pace, readying us for action
- Blood rushes to our arms and legs, preparing us to run fast or stand strong

Note that this system is not only activated when we perceive something as danger; it's also active when we exercise, and in other examples of being in an active state.

The ventral vagal system:
The Green Zone Seeking Connection

The ventral vagal system is the most recent system from an evolutionary standpoint. When this system is active, we seek connection, feeling social and safe. It's what helps us connect with others, share moments, and feel loved; learn new things and explore the world; and calm down after stress and find our balance again. Here our bodies function in optimal form.

System hierarchy

Polyvagal Theory is based on the idea of a fixed hierarchy of these three states, like building blocks that are stacked on top of each other. It is often pictured as a ladder. The lowest (oldest) part of the ladder is referred to as the dorsal vagal system of immobilization; the next building block, halfway up the ladder, is the sympathetic activation system; and the top part of the ladder is the most recent ventral vagal system of social interaction.

This hierarchy explains why we first need some sympathetic energy (gentle movement) to get out of a dorsal vagal state (immobilization) before being able to regulate to the ventral vagal state (calm and connected).

Why is it good to know how to move comfortably between these states? Well, life is full of changes and challenges. One moment we're relaxed, and the next we might need to jump into action. Being able to switch between states easily means we're adaptable and resilient. It's a sign of a well-balanced nervous system. As we learn to navigate these states, we're teaching our nervous system to be more flexible and resilient. It's all about finding that sweet spot of balance, where we can handle stress, enjoy relaxation, and connect deeply with those around us. I call it becoming a **nervous system navigator**.

Both we and our horses experience these shifts many times a day. It's perfectly normal and actually very healthy. However, when we have experienced trauma, we can get stuck in one state, which has an effect on many areas in our life and can even create health problems.

Becoming a nervous system navigator and easily shifting between states is a very useful skill for all aspects in life. It's like practicing a skill; the more we do it, the better we get at moving in and out of stress and finding our balance each time. We will learn in detail about how to do this and increase resilience in Chapter 12.

CHAPTER 6

Neuroception

In this chapter, we go deeper into the concept of neuroception, a term that might sound complicated but is actually something our bodies do all the time without us even thinking about it.

Neuroception is our body's secret agent, always on the lookout for safety or danger in our surroundings. It's part of the autonomic nervous system, which means it works quietly in the background, checking out what's happening around and inside us. This process helps our brain decide whether we're in a safe place, if there's something to worry about, or if we're facing a serious threat.

Neuroception listens to three streams of input: inside (the body), outside (the environment), and between (others' nervous systems).

Imagine you have an internal radar that's always active, scanning for signals that might mean safety or danger. That's **neuroception**. And it all happens without us having to think about it, to prepare us best for possible danger.

Neuroception helps us react to our environment fast. Unlike **perception**, which involves actively thinking about what we see or hear, neuroception works outside of our conscious awareness. It makes very quick decisions about our safety.

When our neuroception senses that everything is okay, we feel calm and relaxed. This calm state makes it easier for us to socialize and deal with day-to-day tasks. Neuroception also picks up on cues that make us feel uneasy or alert, triggering a reaction before we even understand why.

Beyond neuroception: Exteroception, Interoception and Proprioception

To understand our environment and ourselves better, it's helpful to also know the meaning of the related concepts exteroception, interoception and proprioception:

- **Exteroception** focuses on the outside world. It's how we notice sights, sounds, smells, tastes, and things we can touch. Most of the time, this is where we pay the most attention.

- **Interoception** gives us insight into what's happening inside our bodies. It can be about physical sensations, like hunger or pain, or emotions like happiness or anxiety.
- **Proprioception** tells us where our body is in space. It's the sense that lets us move smoothly and know the position of our limbs without looking.

It's fascinating how we can sense something's not right without really knowing why. Horses are especially good at this. They feel the vibes we radiate and respond accordingly. This is based on neuroception. They feel whether or not we are a safe spot for them. You will find practical exercises on how to become a safe spot for your horse in Parts III and IV.

When we feel safe, it's easier to trust. And when we connect with horses, trust is crucial, so neuroception sets the rhythm. Horses are very sensitive to our signals, even those we're not aware of sending. As prey animals, they need to sense (for example) whether that lion is hungry or not.

Paying attention to our own neuroception and cues from our horses is like learning a new language—the language of *safety* and *connection*. Tuning into these subtle signals opens a new level of partnership with our horses.

When neuroception takes input from the external world, we immediately respond with what is called the **orienting response** (OR), also known as the orienting reflex. This is how we and horses react when something in our environment changes, but not so suddenly that it scares us.

Imagine you hear a weird noise or see something move out of the corner of your eye. You turn to look at it, right? That's the OR in action.

This response makes us stop what we're doing for a moment. We may turn our heads, focus our eyes on where we think the change is happening, or even stop moving altogether. Our bodies react too—our heart rate may go up a bit, and our blood vessels open up a little more. This *mix of curiosity and alertness* is all about becoming more aware and ready to move if we need to.

This state is often confused with the freeze response (i.e. the dorsal vagal state), but it's not the same. We will explore that a bit later in the book.

When we have figured out we aren't in danger, we may take a deep sigh and then go back to our normal activities. If the neuroception in the horse decides there's no danger, he just goes back to what he was doing, maybe after showing some signs of calming himself down and releasing tension, like lowering his head or making a soft noise. If something continues to be perceived as dangerous, our bodies get ready to either fight the problem or run away from it. When the danger feels life-threatening, we may freeze and not be able to run away.

CHAPTER 7

The Vagus Nerve

As mentioned, the main reason for the term "Polyvagal Theory" is because the vagus nerve has two branches ("poly-" is a prefix meaning "many"). So what's so special about the vagus nerve?

The vagus nerve, also known as the 10th cranial nerve, is like *a superhighway connecting our brain to many parts of our body*, including our heart, lungs and stomach. It's like a power cable helping our body manage functions such as controlling our heartbeat, blood pressure, digestion, and even how we sweat and speak.

Why should we care about the vagus nerve, especially when thinking about horses? It's all about *emotions* and *connections*. This nerve helps control how we feel by sending messages between the brain and the body. It's crucial for understanding how we feel, whether calm or stressed, and plays a big part in how we connect with others, including our four-legged friends.

As mentioned in the hierarchy ladder, the way animals respond to danger has evolved over time. Initially, creatures like reptiles could only "shut down" to protect themselves. As animals evolved, mammals developed the ability to move quickly away from threats, utilizing a fight-or-flight response.

We humans and other social animals then developed an even more advanced level of this nerve's function. We engage socially without fear, thanks to the ventral vagal system. This means we're built *not just to survive but to connect and bond with others*, which can include our horses. The development of the nervous system mirrors the development of the brain.

The vagus nerve has two main branches that have different tasks:

1. **Ventral vagal branch**—This part originates in the brain and is connected to nerves and other parts of our body in our face, neck and upper chest (the part above the diaphragm). These areas help us smile, talk and listen, which are all important for connecting with others and making friends. Think of the ventral vagal branch as our body's system for bonding and socializing.

2. **Dorsal vagal branch**—This part goes to our belly, lungs, heart and other organs, and helps us relax and digest our food. It also has a special job when things get too scary or overwhelming. It makes us freeze or shut down, almost like hitting the pause button, to help protect us.

Have you ever wondered how we manage to keep our cool in a tricky situation or calm down after something stressful happens? That's all thanks to something called **nervous system regulation**. Simply put, it's our body's way of adjusting to changes and challenges without getting too stressed. It helps us bounce back after tough times, making us feel in control and safe.

The vagus nerve is the peacekeeper of our body. When it's working well, it helps calm things down after a scare by telling our heart to slow down and our muscles to relax. For horse enthusiasts, understanding how the vagus nerve works helps us better connect with our horses. Just like us, horses need a calm and regulated nervous system to feel safe and build trust with their human friends.

By learning about nervous system regulation and the role of the vagus nerve, we can create a more harmonious environment for ourselves and our equine companions. It's all about *building a sense of safety and confidence*, both for ourselves and for the horses we care so much about.

Vagal tone:
The Symphony of Relaxation

When we talk about "vagal tone," think of it as the strength or fitness level of the vagus nerve. Just like a muscle, *the stronger our vagal tone, the easier our body can relax and handle stress.*

A high vagal tone is like having a world-class music conductor making sure everything in our body plays together nicely and in harmony. A relaxed environment is key for both human and equine well-being.

We can actually improve our vagal tone through simple, everyday actions. Some simple things that you can do include:

- **Deep breathing**

Taking slow, deep breaths is one of the easiest ways to tell your vagus nerve, "Hey, it's okay to relax now." Imagine each incoming breath bringing calm, and each outgoing breath releasing tension.

- **Gentle touch**

Gentle strokes or a soothing massage can work wonders for activating the vagus nerve. It's a silent way of saying to your body, "Everything's going to be alright." Give yourself a hug from time to time, and stroke your hands, arms or face.

- **Laughter and joy**

Ever noticed how good you feel after a laugh? That's your vagus nerve enjoying the vibe, too. I've learned to laugh instead of getting frustrated when my horse gives me a different answer than I asked for.

- **Connection and bonding**

Spending quality time with your horse is enjoyable; it strengthens your bond with him and activates the vagus nerve. It's like telling both your and your horse's nervous systems you're in a safe, happy place.

- **Mindful practices**

Engaging in mindfulness, meditation or yoga can really improve your vagal tone. These practices help signal to your body it's time to drop into a state of peace and relaxation.

In Part III I have added ten short, practical strategies on how to boost your vagal tone and regulate yourself.

As we spend time with our horses, making habits of relaxing together is very important. These habits help our body's calm-down nerve kick into action.

With your horse, practice mindful grooming instead of just getting the dirt off. Hang out together without doing anything, read a book in the pasture, or walk next to your horse during part of your trail ride. These kinds of activities tell you and your horse it's okay to relax.

Making these calming activities a regular part of your day is both good for yourself and makes your bond with your horse even stronger.

Understanding the vagus nerve makes a world of difference by helping us see how our bodies are wired to handle stress, danger and social interactions. As we recognize these signals in ourselves and our equine partners, we now have tools to activate the vagus nerve, creating a safer, more connected environment.

Next time you're interacting with a horse, remember the power of the vagus nerve.

CHAPTER 8

Window of Tolerance

The **Window of Tolerance** is a term introduced by Daniel J. Siegel in 1999, a clinical professor of psychiatry. The "window" describes the optimal emotional zone where we can best function and thrive in everyday life. This concept helps explain how our feelings go up and down all the time. The aim is to stay within the Window of Tolerance, which will be explained in this chapter.

When you're feeling a certain level of stress, and you are able to regulate yourself into relaxation again, you're in your Window of Tolerance. This means you're in a sweet spot where you can handle challenges without losing your cool. Your Window of Tolerance is characterized by a sense of openness, flexibility, curiosity and presence, and a capacity to cope with life's daily triggers. Within your window you can:

- Think clearly
- Understand how you and others feel
- Try new things and learn
- Express your emotions in a way that suits the event

Even when something stressful happens, you can manage these things well.

What if the stress level gets too high or sticks around too long? That's when things can get tricky, and you might find yourself either above or below the Window of Tolerance. The zones above or below the optimal zone are called the **hyperarousal** zone (too much activation) and the **hypoarousal** zone (too little activation).

Hyperarousal is when you are on high alert, sometimes without even noticing it. Maybe you're snappy, very tense, or just can't seem to relax. This could be because of a stressful event that keeps you worrying, or a lingering reaction to early childhood events as we discussed in Chapter 3. In hyperarousal it's hard to see things clearly or get along well with others.

On the flip side, when you're in a state of hypoarousal, you can feel empty and numb, or maybe don't have the energy to care about anything. It's like being stuck in a fog.

We already learned that when you feel stressed, your survival mechanism kicks in to protect you. It gets ready to fight, flee or freeze. Once the danger passes, your body calms down; your heart rate slows down, your muscles relax, and everything goes back to normal. If stress stays within your Window of Tolerance, you're okay. But if stress overflows this window on either side and keeps going, it's not good. It can wear you out or even make you ill over time (we'll explore that more in the next chapter).

When you search for "Window of Tolerance" on the internet, you will mostly find illustrations with three layers: within the window (ventral vagal), above the window (hyperarousal or sympathetic) and below the window (hypoarousal or dorsal vagal). Since I wanted to indicate that the sympathetic and dorsal vagal state are also within the window *as long as we feel safe,* I have adjusted it to a five-zone map of the Window of Tolerance.

The first three illustrations show a healthy movement through the various states of the nervous system, staying within the Window of Tolerance, whereas the last two illustrations show a state of hyperarousal and hypoarousal, being outside of the Window of Tolerance.

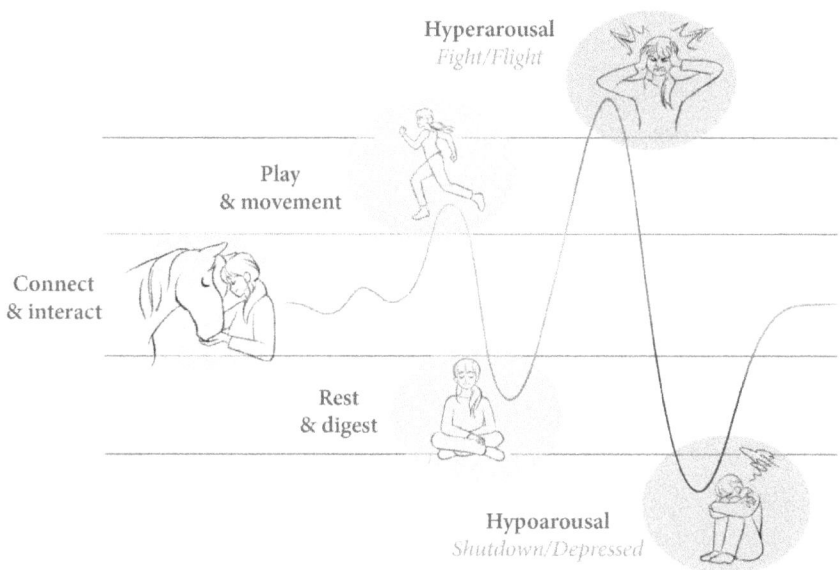

Knowing your Window of Tolerance allows you to understand your emotional world. When you are within this zone, things are balanced. It feels like you're in a cozy place where you can be a lighthouse of calm for your horse. And yes, your horse can tell when you're in this spot and feels more at ease, too.

It's great to understand how to keep your emotions in a range that's good for you and your horse, because horses are very aware of how we feel. When we're calm and in our Window of Tolerance, they feel our peace and will be calmer, too. But if we get too stressed or check out, they notice that as well and may get jumpy or move away from us.

The good news is that we can practice and get better at keeping ourselves in this happy, optimal zone. As we already learned, things like deep breathing, paying attention to the moment, and gentle touches can help us guide our feelings back into the green zone.

CHAPTER 9

The Faux Window

As mentioned in the previous chapter, there is actually a name for being in a state of hyper- or hypoarousal for a longer period of time without realizing it. When you seem relaxed on the outside but aren't on the inside, you could be navigating in something called the **faux window**.

When you live with sustained activation of your nervous system for a prolonged period of time, your body and mind adapt to it. It becomes your new normal and you no longer notice that you're actually in a stressed zone. Your body and mind now believe that this level of activation is necessary for everyday life. From the outside, you may look cool and collected. However, that's because you've learned certain patterns or habits, often unconsciously, to seem in control even when you're stressed.

There are many ways this expresses itself. Some main indications that you're living in a faux window include moodiness, intolerance, constantly moving, trouble sleeping, stomach and digestion problems, relationship conflict, emotional eating, and others. Imagine someone who's always busy, working all the time, or someone who tries to do everything perfectly. They may look as if they've got it all under control, but inside they're in survival mode. Instead of being in their comfort zone, they are in their faux window.

In our world, being busy or disconnected from how we truly feel is often seen as normal. But as mentioned above, missing the signs of being in your faux window can lead to problems.

Coping strategies

People instinctively try to deal with tough situations they find themselves in. They develop strategies to handle feelings of fear or anxiety, which may involve working hard to avoid these feelings.

This isn't a wrong strategy. They're dealing with life's challenges the best way they know how, and these strategies help them survive tough times. However, things may have changed in their life, making these strategies no longer useful or beneficial to their well-being.

Finding safe, healthy ways to deal with stress helps us get back into our true comfort zone. This may mean learning new coping skills or finding someone to talk with about our feelings.

When your stress alarm system seems too sensitive, getting set off by things that aren't really threats, your Window of Tolerance has become very small. You may be living in a faux window, making it harder to deal with stress.

As we discussed in Chapter 3 on trauma, early childhood experiences have an impact on the development of your nervous system, which can make your Window of Tolerance shrink. This means you may feel upset or thrown off-balance more easily.

Are you feeling like you're always on high alert? Wanting to keep control? Trying to be perfect all the time? Or do you check out easily? These are signs that you have a small Window of Tolerance. You aren't alone.

As I mentioned before, this is not a book on trauma and I am not a therapist. On a personal note, I had to learn the hard way that my body was stuck in trauma. People always commented on how smart I was, how confident I looked, how amazing I was for traveling all over the world. But trying to always be perfect, being on high alert, performing at 200 percent all the time, all wore me out. Just because someone looks peaceful on the outside doesn't mean they're feeling peaceful on the inside. As I often say, *not all stillness is calm.*

If you recognize any of these signals in yourself, find support. There's nothing wrong with going to a therapist. Find someone who's not only interacting with your cognitive brain, but also works with your body and nervous system (known as the somatic approach).

In short, it's okay to have certain coping or management strategies; however, don't let these take over your life! They're part of who you are and how you've learned to cope with the world around you. The key is to understand why you have them, so you can consciously decide when and how to use them best. This understanding will help you and your animals find your way back to a balanced and comfortable state where you can truly thrive.

CHAPTER 10

What's Your Story?

Understanding where you are in your nervous system can be like reading a map while on a journey. The nervous system sends signals from your body to your brain, and you tell your stories and express your behaviors and feelings based on that information.

First, let's figure out what each state feels like for you. This is about finding words that capture how you feel in different states. By becoming an observer and listening to your stories and body sensations, you can identify which state you're in.

Our emotional states each come with their own narrative. If we step back and listen to our internal stories, they will guide us to understand our current state.

- **Fight/Flight (sympathetic)**

When your sympathetic system is activated, your stories may say the world is a scary place, filled with danger. These stories drive you to act, often pushing you into overdrive as you try to stay safe. You may use words like "worried," "stressed" or "overwhelmed" to describe this state.

- **Freeze (dorsal vagal)**

In the dorsal vagal state, your stories may tell you things are hopeless, nothing will change, and you're all alone. These thoughts can make you feel stuck and disconnected. Words like "numb" or "shutdown" describe this state.

- **Safe and social (ventral vagal)**

Positive stories thrive in the ventral vagal state, telling you life is good and you are safe. This state allows you to connect with others and feel open. Words like "happy," "content" or "joyful" fit here.

Why observe our emotions? Because knowing the words that match your feelings helps you quickly understand which state you're in. This awareness is key to managing your emotions and state better.

The state you're in affects everything. Not knowing your state leaves you stuck. By becoming aware of your current state, recognizing where you want to be, and practicing ways to get there, you can change your perspective and, ultimately, your life.

To understand the profound impact of your state on your life, think of a single experience and write three different stories about it, each from the perspective of one of your nervous system states—dorsal (freeze), sympathetic (fight/flight), and ventral (safe and social).

Example: Struggling to open a can of food

- **Sympathetic state story:** *"This is infuriating! Why would they make a can that's impossible to open? Don't they think about their customers at all? Every time I try to do something simple, it turns into a disaster."*
- **Dorsal state story:** *"I'm too weak to open this can. It's hopeless. I'll never get it open, and I'm going to be left hungry. This always happens. I'm just too old and incapable."*
- **Ventral state story:** *"Okay, this can is a bit tricky to open. Let's see...maybe there's a tool that can help, or perhaps there's another snack I can enjoy instead. No big deal, I'll figure it out."*

What is *your* story? And how would it feel if you consciously *choose* your story?

Change your story and you'll change your life!

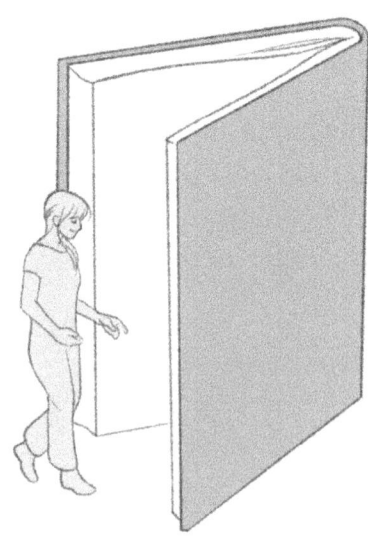

50

From awareness to transformation

The first step in this process is awareness. By observing and acknowledging the state you're currently in, you begin the process of transformation. This awareness allows you to appreciate your nervous system's attempt to protect you, whether through connection (ventral) or protection (sympathetic/dorsal), based on your brain's perception of safety or threat.

Next, think about what triggers these states and what brings you back to feeling good. They're known by the common names **triggers** and **glimmers**.

- **Triggers** are experiences that push you into fight, flight or freeze. It could be an argument, a bad day at work, or even getting cut off in traffic. Write these down so you know what to watch out for.
- **Glimmers** are things you can do to help you feel safe and calm. The term was introduced by Deb Dana in her 2018 book *The Polyvagal Theory in Therapy*. Maybe it's petting a dog, grooming your horse or chatting with a friend. Recognizing these will help you find your way back to a place where you feel calm and safe.

Simply put: Awareness + Action + Repetition = Transformation.

By identifying your emotional states, recognizing your triggers, and knowing what brings you joy, you take a big step towards understanding yourself better. This self-awareness allows you to regulate your emotions and respond to stress in healthier ways. Once you're aware of your state, you can start to question the story your brain has created about your experience. Is there

51

another way to look at this situation? Can you shift from a story of protection and survival to one of connection and resilience?

By consciously choosing to view your experience from a different state, you change the narrative. This doesn't mean dismissing or invalidating your feelings, but rather understanding them as part of a broader range of responses.

Acceptance and humor

The ventral state story often involves acceptance and humor, tools that will shift your perspective. In the example above of opening the can, moving to a ventral state means accepting the challenge and finding humor in the situation, transforming frustration into a moment of lightness and creativity. This is what I do with horses. When they give a different response than I anticipated, I laugh instead of getting frustrated. I have rewired my brain to do this automatically, without thinking about it. It often surprises people when they see me laugh after my horse acts up or walks away.

Remember, your emotional state shapes your story, which in turn shapes your life. By practicing awareness and flexibility, you will navigate life's challenges with more grace and resilience, and become an accomplished nervous system navigator. Appreciate your nervous system for its protective efforts; and remember, you have the power to change your state, change your story, and ultimately change your life.

CHAPTER 11

Neuroplasticity

Our brains constantly change based on our life events and our responses to them. The cells of our brain and nervous system have arm-like extensions called **dendrites**. Think of your brain like a forest that grows roots and branches to communicate with each other. Just as a forest will grow and change over time, so will your brain. This incredible ability of the brain to adapt and transform throughout your life is called **neuroplasticity**. You can say it's like the brain's superpower to heal, learn and evolve.

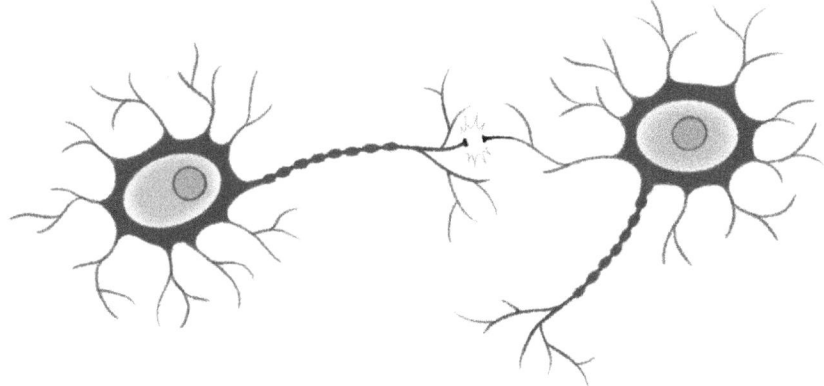

To dive in deeper, we need to talk about **synaptic plasticity**. In this case, think of paths that are walked on every day by a group of animals, going to a river to drink water by using the easiest route possible. Over time, the grass and dirt along these paths become trampled down, making them clearer to see and easier to travel. This is like how our brain evolves with learning and experience.

Every time we learn something new, our brain builds a path by connecting neurons (i.e. our brain cells). These paths help us remember and use what we've learned while using less effort each time. The more you revisit this information, the more you practice, the stronger and clearer the path becomes.

When neurons communicate through these pathways, they use tiny gaps called synapses. Every time you use a pathway, the communication across these synapses gets better, making it easier for the brain to process and recall information. This is synaptic plasticity in action—it's the foundation of how we learn and remember things.

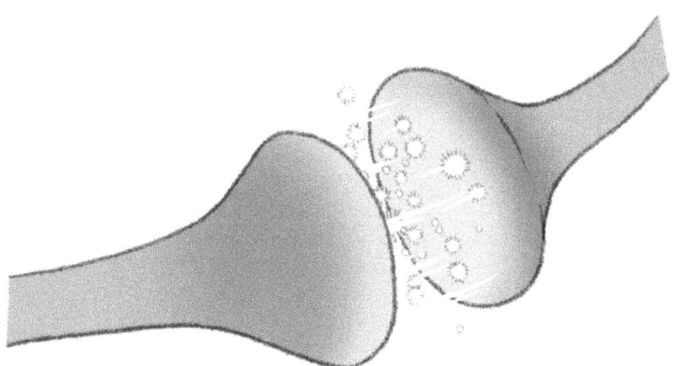

Neuroplasticity can be life-saving because, even after head injuries or neurological conditions, our brain will find new ways to recover and adjust. Similarly, neuroplasticity gives us a way out when we feel like we're stuck in a certain habit or pattern, and are feeling stressed all the time. When we do things that relax us, we are rewiring our brains for health and stepping off the stress train.

Neuroplasticity shows us change is always possible. No matter the challenges we face—be it injury, illness, or learning new skills— our brains have the remarkable capacity to adapt and create new pathways. However, *repetition is key* to neuroplasticity. The more we practice being calm, the more our brain gets the message and makes it a habit.

This change benefits you and your horse. Horses pick up on how we feel. As you become more centered and calm, you invite your horse into a peaceful space, deepening your connection. In simple terms, by understanding and working with your nervous system, you guide your body toward a state of calm and well-being, making life a bit easier and more enjoyable, for both yourself and your horse.

Remember—what fires together, wires together.

CHAPTER 12

Increasing Resilience

Resilience is your ability to bounce back after a hard day or other challenging situations. It's about growing stronger even when things get tough. It's like being a boat in a stormy sea; even when the waves come crashing down, you manage to stay afloat and navigate through them. It's about adapting well to tough times or stress. This doesn't just happen overnight; it needs practice like building muscle. You get stronger with practice.

Moreover, being resilient means having a *set of skills* that help you cope. It's about finding ways to solve problems, and knowing how to calm yourself when you're upset. It's about smoothly moving between different states of your nervous system.

It's important to remember, being resilient doesn't mean you won't feel stressed or upset anymore. Everyone feels stressed sometimes. What matters is how you deal with those feelings.

To become more resilient means training your brain like you would a muscle. The steps include:

1. Find your stress simulators (triggers)

Look for activities that challenge you but don't put you at risk of harm. Anything that gently triggers your sympathetic nervous system can work. It's like exercising your stretch zone without going into the stress zone. This could be physical, like doing a short strenuous exercise or taking a cold shower. It could also be something that makes you a bit nervous, like being in a crowded place or speaking in public.

2. Notice your response

Pay attention when you start feeling stressed. What are the physical signs? Is your heartbeat going up? Do you get a dry throat? Do you start sweating? It's important to notice the initial signs, so you can acknowledge them in an actual challenging situation.

3. Practice switching between states

Then consciously move from feeling a little stressed (sympathetic nervous system) to feeling calm (parasympathetic nervous system). Part III of this book will give you ten strategies for bringing yourself back to a calm state. The more you do this when you're safe, the better you'll get at it. Now you have a new option when you find yourself in a challenging situation.

Building resilience is like learning to ride the waves of life. By understanding how your nervous system works and practicing how to regulate it, you're equipping yourself with the tools to navigate life's challenges more smoothly. Remember, every time you face a fear or stressor head-on, especially in a safe environment, you're taking steps to strengthen your resilience.

You're creating new synaptic pathways in your brain. So instead of dreading your challenges, start to look forward to them! See them as your next opportunity to enhance your brain and become more resilient over time.

You now have a good understanding of Polyvagal Theory. In Part II, coming next, we will see how we can translate the polyvagal principles into practical lessons for training our horse.

PART II

Polyvagal Principles Applied to Horse Training

In this part of the book, we look at how Polyvagal Theory is translated into working with horses, especially horses that have experienced negative events or even trauma in their life.

CHAPTER 13

The Horse-Human Relationship

In this chapter, we look at the horse-human relationship, viewed through the lens of Polyvagal Theory. This theory helps us understand how deeply horses can connect with us, sensing our emotions and mirroring our nervous system states.

Horses have an incredible ability to read human emotions. They feel what we're feeling, without us having to say a word. Their sensitivity allows them to respond to our emotional state and intentions, a key survival tool when encountering a predator.

There's a special kind of interaction between horses and humans. Our nervous systems can influence each other. In training and interacting with horses, creating a sense of safety and trust is crucial. By co-regulating, we help each other stay balanced and calm. It's about building a relationship where both you and your horse feel secure and understood.

I believe that *you can only connect with your horse if you are connected to yourself.* What does this mean? It means being in an embodied state, where you are connected to the sensations of your body. In this state, you feel confident and safe, which is reflected in your posture and presence. You're open to listening to your inner wisdom, and you trust your intuition. Your heart and mind work together harmoniously in a coherent way, and your outer state reflects your inner state.

Coherence is when everything in your body functions optimally. This is closely linked to your **heart rate variability (HRV)**, which changes with your emotions. Fear can disrupt coherence, but by shifting to feelings of trust and love, you can create a smooth, wave-like pattern in your HRV. This state of coherence emits a powerful, positive energy that horses are naturally drawn to. It's like tuning into a radio frequency that horses love.

Negative emotions like frustration and anxiety make your heart rhythms erratic, while positive feelings like gratitude and love promote coherence. By choosing to focus on and embody these positive emotions, you can change your heart's rhythm and the energy you emit.

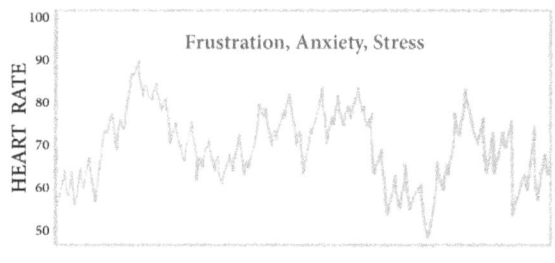

Incoherent heart rhythm pattern

Stressful negative attitudes and emotions, like frustration and anxiety cause chaotic heart rhythms, leading to increased cortisol levels and disruptive sleep rhythms.

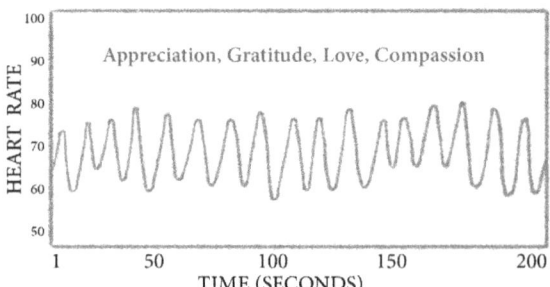

Coherent heart rhythm pattern

Positive attitudes and emotions, like appreciation, create smooth coherent heart rhythms, leading to more restful and revitalizing sleep

Copyright 2009 Institute of HeartMath

62

Daring to open your heart and express your true self will transform your relationship with your horse. When you choose to embody love and gratitude, you create a coherent state that makes your horse feel safe and connected to you.

Remember, communication with your horse is most effective when it comes from a place of gratitude and coherence. Instead of demanding, *ask* your horse to do something and express your thanks. It strengthens your bond and supports both of you getting into a state of heart coherence.

What if your horse isn't responding as expected when you ask a question? It's crucial to approach this with understanding and curiosity rather than frustration. Try the following steps:

- *Check for physical issues.* Tight muscles could be a response to pain or injury. However, they can also result from the horse's brain signaling the body to tense up because he expects to be hurt, either because of an old injury or because of previous experiences.
- *Ensure a sense of safety.* Your horse must feel safe to relax. Chronic tension is a sign of discomfort that needs addressing.
- *Understand the brain.* Recent research into equine neuroscience offers invaluable insights. Knowing how a horse's nervous system works enables you to train and interact in ways that respect their natural instincts and needs.

Herd dynamics and co-regulation

Have you ever noticed a group of horses seeming to move and react as one? This is because horses are incredibly social animals. They're connected through their energy field. For them, being part of a herd is not just about companionship; it's about survival. In the wild, their safety and life depend on being able to communicate quickly and effectively about perceived danger.

This concept of nervous systems that adapt to each other, which we've seen applied to humans in Polyvagal Theory, is just as crucial in the horse world. Horses constantly adjust their behavior based on the signals they receive from their herd mates. If one horse becomes alert to a potential threat, others will pick up on this and become alert too. Conversely, if a horse signals that all is well, this will help calm others. We humans can also consciously radiate to our horse that all is well, and help calm them.

While we humans rely heavily on words to communicate, horses use body language and energy. They are experts at reading the slightest changes in posture, expression and movement. So as horse enthusiasts, we need to become students of equine body language. Learning to read and respond to what your horse is "saying" through his body language will deepen your connection. Small signs, like the position of their ears or the tension in their body, will tell you a lot about what they're feeling.

Why is this important? Because when they feel safe, they're more open to exploring, asking questions, and forming genuine connections. Safety nurtures a learning frame of mind. It's a mental space where you and your horse are ready to learn together, because you both feel comfortable and open. This environment invites curiosity rather than fear, making learning a joyful experience.

Creating a safe environment is a shared responsibility. Being consistent and reliable in our actions helps build this mutual trust. When safety leads the way, learning together becomes an exciting adventure. In a safe space, there's room to try, fail and grow without fear. This approach turns the learning process into a shared journey of discovery.

By applying what we know from Polyvagal Theory, we will better understand how to create a space of safety and connection with our horses. Recognizing when they're feeling stressed and knowing how to respond can turn potential conflicts and tension into moments of bonding. When we learn to respect and respond to the unique ways horses communicate and regulate their emotions, we create a partnership based on mutual trust and understanding.

CHAPTER 14

How Horses Learn

The human brain and horse brain are structured differently. In this chapter we discuss the different ways of perception and learning in horses and humans.

The human brain is about 1/50th of the total body weight. For the horse, it is about 1/500th. Aside from size and percentage of total body weight, the biggest difference between human and horse brains is the size of the cerebellum and the prefrontal cortex.

The cerebellum (also known as the "small brain") is the area of the brain where balance and movement are coordinated. For humans this part is about one-fifth of the total brain, while for horses it's about one-third, which is logical considering that horses are first and foremost driven by movement.

As we learned in Part I, the prefrontal cortex handles tasks like logical thinking, making plans, and controlling impulses. Humans can think ahead, strategize, and control their fear responses, and they also have the ability to deceive. Horses, however, don't have this capability in the same way we do. Their response is always 100% honest. Horses don't "do things on purpose" or understand concepts like "winning," because their prefrontal cortex doesn't work like ours.

Instead, when horses receive sensory information, they react almost instantly. This immediate reaction is crucial for survival in the wild, where taking time to ponder could mean life or death. When we face what seems like misbehavior in the horse, it's often an expression of uncertainty or fear. Every response the horse gives is essentially asking, "Am I safe?" Recognizing this can transform our approach to training and interaction.

How should we respond? By being a source of calm and assurance. Our role is to communicate safety, helping our horses shift from a state of stress to one of relaxation and trust where they feel safe.

You may be familiar with training techniques involving pressure and release, where it's mentioned that "pressure motivates and the release teaches." However, it's not the release itself, it's the pause after the release that constitutes the critical moment in the learning process. This pause is when the magic happens in the horse's brain. It allows for the creation of new neural pathways and the storage of new information.

Consolidation

A horse's brain "replays" the activities performed before the pause. Repetition strengthens the neural pathways that are being activated, making certain behaviors more fluent over time. This process is called **consolidation**, when sensory input and activities are linked with other similar pathways in the brain. This encourages the growth of dendrites, indicating the brain is actively learning.

Do you know that moment when someone mentions something and you think, "That sounds like something else I've heard before?" When you take a break, you suddenly realize the link between both events. That's the process of consolidation. New events are linked or associated in the brain for long-term memory.

A good night's sleep helps quite a bit with this consolidation, as it's during sleep that new information is re-arranged so that it can be better retrieved the next day. Sleep is crucial for horses as well. A lot of horses suffer from sleep deprivation, as they're kept in a small stall for too many hours where they can't lie flat on their side. Horses can rest lying on their sternum, but they can only access REM sleep when they lie down.

To keep your horse in a state conducive to learning, it's essential to spark their curiosity and give them time to figure things out, and for the brain to consolidate. Bombarding your horse with commands or questions without sufficient breaks will lead to anxiety, shifting them into a fight, flight or even freeze mode, where learning becomes impossible. We should make sure training sessions include pauses for the horse to relax and process, and avoid overwhelming pressure.

We're all energy beings. Horses are incredibly sensitive to our emotions and intentions. They sense whether we're calm or stressed, which affects their emotional state. So be a safe place for your horse!

CHAPTER 15

Window of Tolerance for Horses

This chapter shows how the Window of Tolerance, the theory that Daniel Siegel originally intended for humans, can be translated to horses. When horses are within the Window of Tolerance, they feel safe and can function optimally.

In Part I we looked at how the three main nervous system states manifest in humans. Let's now look at the three main states of the horse's nervous system, and how it can be seen in their behavior:

The sympathetic state: Fight or Flight

The sympathetic state is when the fight-or-flight response is triggered. Horses show an increased heart rate, fast and shallow breathing, and tense muscles.

The ventral vagal state: Calm and Connected

In the ventral vagal state, horses are relaxed, attentive and ready to connect. Their eyes are soft, their breathing is relaxed and rhythmic, and they are curious, showing a willingness to connect and engage.

The dorsal vagal state:
Shutdown or Dissociated

When horses are overwhelmed and see no way out, they might enter the dorsal vagal state, a shutdown response. You will see a lack of responsiveness, glazed eyes, a stiff, immobile stance, and a disconnect from their surroundings.

When I was looking for ways to apply the polyvagal principles and incorporate the Window of Tolerance into my horse training, just referring to these three states felt limiting. For example, we do need some activity and arousal when we want to go for a canter, or explain new side movements to our horse. As long as they feel safe, this is okay! That's why, similar to humans, we distinguish a safe (green) and unsafe (red) perspective for both the sympathetic and dorsal vagal state of a horse.

Red sympathetic state:
Fight or Flight [Hyperarousal]

When horses perceive danger, their survival mode is activated. This isn't just about running from predators (or plastic bags), it's also when we ask too much of our horse, when we escalate pressure, or we ask too many questions. Being in this high-alert mode for a long period of time has an effect on many aspects in a horse, like health issues and compromised movement.

Green sympathetic state:
Active and Playful

When safety isn't an issue, this state is all about activation and movement. Horses become lively and ready to play, run and jump. It's the joy of movement and learning, where a little bit of excitement fuels training and new learning. Your horse may shake his mane and give you a piaffe or levade by himself. The heart rate goes up, muscles tighten, and breathing deepens. From fun and games it can go to a fight-or-flight response; it's all about how intense the situation feels.

Green ventral vagal state: Calm and Connected

This is a calm place, where feeling safe and social interactions are the main priorities. Horses seek social interaction with other horses (or with their human), regulating one another through closeness or appeasement. Their heart beats calmly, they breathe easily, and their muscles are relaxed. This is when the ventral vagus system puts a gentle "brake" on the rest of the ANS. Training begins in this space of mutual respect and understanding. For a horse to learn and connect, relaxation isn't just helpful; it's essential.

Green dorsal vagal state: Rest and Digest

In this state, everything is calm and relaxed. It's a time for resting, digesting, gentle interactions, grazing or grooming. They may hang out, groom each other, or enjoy a leisurely graze. Their heart rate is low, breathing is steady, and muscles are relaxed. It's a beautiful feeling to relax together with your horse and just do nothing.

Red dorsal vagal state: Immobilized [Hypoarousal]

When horses perceive great danger and escape seems impossible, horses can go into shutdown mode. Their heart rate drops, breathing slows, and the horse can even seem frozen. It's a conservation mode, like bears that hibernate to save energy during the cold winter months. It's a survival trick from nature. It narrows the awareness and even the senses, so they won't feel the pain of a possible death. This is their body's emergency brake, dominated by the dorsal vagal system. Sometimes, when a horse feels it can't change its situation, it may seem that he isn't responding to your aids. This isn't because he's lazy; it's because he's stuck in this low-energy state, feeling helpless.

Learning about the Window of Tolerance and how to recognize these various states will enhance our training and relationship with our horses. The first three images in the following illustration indicate a horse within his Window of Tolerance, whereas the last two drawings show a horse in hyperarousal and hypoarousal.

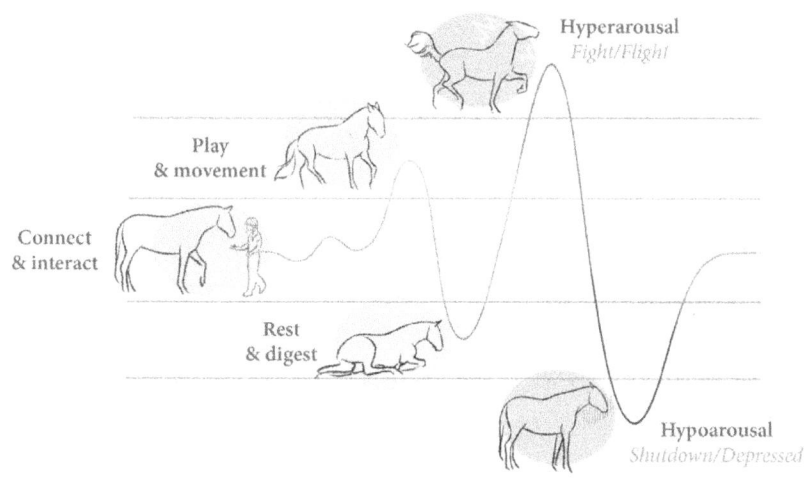

Reading your horse's nervous system

Horses, by nature, are social beings. They first seek connection—looking to their herd, or to us as their handler, for communication and support. If they feel unsupported or face an immediate threat, their response escalates to fight or flight. And in extreme distress, they may shut down entirely.

Incorporating insights from Polyvagal Theory into our approach to horse training offers a groundbreaking new perspective. It enables us to recognize and respect the natural responses of our equine partners. By doing so, we not only foster a safer environment, we also build a foundation for a more empathetic and effective partnership and create optimal learning conditions.

When a horse operates within their Window of Tolerance (the green zones), he is genuinely comfortable with the world around him. This comfort level means he's more receptive to training, more engaged with his human partner, and happier and healthier overall. For example, a relaxed horse will carry his back more comfortably, allowing for a smoother ride. His mind is also more open to learning and adapting to new situations.

We learned that when a horse is stressed, he enters a state that is focused on survival. This means his ability to learn is significantly reduced. His nervous system prioritizes immediate safety over connection and learning.

By understanding and respecting the Window of Tolerance, we create a nurturing environment for our horse. A horse that feels understood and supported is a horse that's ready to connect, learn and thrive.

CHAPTER 16

My Story: Jajão and the ANS

Let me share with you the journey of my horse Jajão and his path through the autonomic nervous system. Drawing upon the foundational concepts introduced in previous chapters, such as Polyvagal Theory and the Window of Tolerance, this chapter offers a personal recounting of how Jajão navigated through the states of the ANS, from shutdown to flight and fight, and eventually towards trust and connection. To remind you, you can visit the link shared at the beginning of the book to see these steps in action.

When Jajão first arrived, his behavior was puzzling. When I would let him free in the arena, he would often retreat to a corner and stand motionless, a sign of going into a shutdown state. I knew I had to use gentle activation to get him out of shutdown mode.

To encourage Jajão to leave his corner, I focused on inviting him to move while making it easy for him. Understanding his inclination to move in the direction he was facing, I ensured there was ample space for him to do so. By creating a bit of energy opposite to where he was looking, I gently nudged him out of his corner. It was fascinating to watch him navigate this process, often moving to another corner as if seeking another safe spot.

75

Listening isn't just about waiting for an audible sound; it's about observing physical signs, and paying attention to any energetic feelings you have about your horse. It's about recognizing the state your horse is in.

Jajão's behavior—standing with his head in the corner or facing the wall—suggested he was dissociating, a term used to describe a disconnection from the present moment, often used as a coping mechanism. This behavior likely stemmed from his past experiences. By gently inviting movement and observing his reactions, I worked to bring him back into a state of awareness and connection.

Approaching Jajão with gentle invitations to interact—asking if I could touch him or if he wanted to go for a walk—allowed him to have a choice. I noticed the softening in his eyes and the slight tremble in his lips, signs he was processing and considering the interaction. As he began to breathe more deeply, I knew he was starting to relax and become more present.

The initial stages of our interaction were all about building connection and communication. I mirrored Jajão's actions, showing interest in what caught his attention, like looking in the same direction or directing my attention to something he was sniffing. This mirroring wasn't just about mimicry; it was an attempt to connect, to say, "I see you, and I'm here with you."

A crucial principle in working with Jajão was ensuring I never cornered him, so he would always feel there was a direction where he could move away from me. Creating a sense of safety meant always allowing him the choice to move away or come closer and interact at his pace.

Moments of connection

Over time, these interactions began to show moments of genuine connection. Initially, I would approach and say hi, and then walk away again. Gradually Jajão would take the initiative to come closer. This dance of approaching and retreating helped build trust, with each encounter bringing us closer.

Working at liberty with Jajão wasn't about keeping him by my side but rather about allowing him the freedom to explore and express himself, and about gathering information. Our sessions often involved me approaching and walking away again, giving him time to process. It was about observing his response, encouraging movement, and then giving him the space to choose his path. This approach wasn't about strict routines. Instead, it was about moving in the moment into a relationship based on mutual respect and understanding. Granting him the freedom to express himself, even if it meant moving away, fostered trust and understanding, acknowledging that connection doesn't require physical closeness at all times.

By consciously slowing down, grounding myself, and exhaling deeply, I worked to communicate calmness and safety. This simple act of breathing out and dropping all energy served as a non-verbal cue to Jajão, inviting him to mirror this state of relaxation and enter a ventral vagal state of connection.

I practiced a state of heart coherence, synchronizing the head and the heart and radiating a harmonious rhythm in my energy field (for more details how to do this, see Chapter 24). By focusing on my heart and radiating feelings of appreciation and love towards Jajão, I communicated care and safety to him. Even when he looked away, signaling he wasn't ready to engage fully, I continued to tell him how amazing he is and that I would give him the time he needed.

Exploring preferences and gathering information

Playing at liberty also made Jajão's preferences become apparent, such as his inclination to move to the right instead of to the left. I did not correct him or restrict his choice. Instead, I viewed these moments as valuable insights into his physical state, as well as the state of his mind and heart.

Even when Jajão's behavior suggested a readiness to attack, I remained composed, knowing that aggression was not his intention. I was curious as to why he felt the need to protect himself. However, I did protect my personal space with energetic or physical boundaries (more on boundaries in Chapter 40).This understanding allowed me to guide him back into movement without fear or anger, emphasizing the importance of compassion and empathy in our interactions.

I used a pointing device (in industry terms called a whip) as a gentle reminder of my space, not as a means of intimidation. A light tap on the ground acts as a cue, reinforcing the importance of my personal space while maintaining a calm demeanor. "You are so gorgeous," I reminded him, acknowledging his beauty and presence despite the challenge.

It's these observations that guide our interactions, prompting gentle inquiries like, "Can we trot? Can you stay with me?" Even when Jajão chose not to stay, my response was one of understanding: "That's fine. Can we maybe change directions?"

Bringing him back into the Window of Tolerance involved his freedom of choice, but also gentle scratches, shared quiet moments, and the reassurance of our bond. "Are we still fine together?"

Every time Jajão drifted away or focused on something else, like another horse, I asked, "Can you stay with me?" It was about finding the sweet spot where he felt comfortable and connected. As Jajão began to relax, his head lowered, signaling trust and contentment. Even when he widened the circle, it was a sign of exploration within the safety of our connection. This, to me, embodies true liberty, my horse choosing to connect because he feels safe and understood.

True liberty means recognizing that "yes" is meaningful only if "no" is an option. When Jajão chooses to be by my side, it's a decision I cherish deeply. It's a testament to trust, a bond forged through mutual respect and understanding.

CHAPTER 17

5xF: Flight, Fight, Fawn, Freeze, Faint

We've talked about the fight/flight/freeze response, but there are actually two more possible responses, *fawn* and *faint*. Let's explore how these instinctive reactions play a role in a horse's survival response.

Flight: The First Line of Survival

Horses are born runners. Their first instinct when faced with danger is to flee, so when there is an escape possible, they will run. This can mean galloping away at full speed or simply avoiding capture.

Fight: When Flight isn't an Option

If escape isn't possible, horses will defend themselves. They might bite, kick or rear, whatever it takes to fend off a threat. While domestication has removed many predators from their lives, this fight response is hardwired into their DNA.

Freeze: Immobility as a Defense

Freezing is hitting the pause button when in a state of fear. When a predator is near, staying still might make a prey less noticeable.

Fawn: Seeking Safety Through Submission

Fawning might seem out of place for horses. Think of it as trying to blend in or appease. A horse may show submissive behavior to avoid conflict or punishment, much like how some humans act to avoid further aggression. Some people see these horses as "calm and well-behaved;" but when you look closer, you see that there's no spirit anymore in the horse, as if nobody's home.

Is this the same as learned helplessness? Not exactly. While both involve a kind of submission, fawning is more about active appeasement, whereas learned helplessness is about giving up when escape seems impossible.

Faint: Tonic Immobility as Final Resource

If the threat escalates, a horse may enter tonic immobility or "faint." While freezing is about stopping in anticipation, fainting is a last-resort defense during an attack, one where the body may fully collapse.

Let's look at trailer loading as an example of these five responses. The first response of most horses is to try to get away from that scary, dark box (flight). When they can't get away, they may try to jump off the ramp, maybe even rear (fight). Then ropes are put behind the butt of the horse and now the horse may not be moving an inch anymore (freeze). Then someone wants to be smart and hits the horse with a broom, and the horse collapses as he thinks he's going to die (faint). The horse realizes the pressure will just continue escalating, and that he can't go anywhere. Next time, he may go into the trailer, appeasing and submissive (fawn).

Orienting response, freeze response, and tonic immobility

Have you ever wondered why a horse suddenly stands as still as a statue, even when there seems to be no immediate danger? This behavior is known as orienting reflex, which we discussed in Chapter 6. This happens when a horse feels a potential threat, yet the danger isn't right on top of him. It's like he's pressing the pause button. That state allows him to be super alert and ready to react without bringing attention to himself. The freeze response is also a pause button; however, in this state he experiences severe threat.

So, how can you tell these apart? Here's a quick guide:

Orienting is when a horse focuses on something new. Neuroception doesn't perceive a serious threat, so the horse is curious but cautious. This response fades as he gets used to the stimulus.

Freezing is about being ready to act. Now neuroception does perceive something as a possible threat. The horse is alert and tense, prepared to bolt or fight if needed.

A state of tonic immobility, on the other hand, is only entered into when the horse feels there's no way to escape danger. The brain perceives a life threat.

People may see their horse act out and say, "My horse exploded out of nowhere." Understanding the above mentioned differences will help you see things from the horse's perspective. You can better support him through stressful situations by recognizing what state the horse is in. For example, if a horse is orienting, you can give him time to explore and become comfortable with the new stimulus. If he's freezing, you know he's feeling threatened and you can help move him away from the possible danger, position yourself between the horse and the perceived danger, or increase the distance when you are the source of tension.

Next time you see a horse standing still, take a moment to observe. Is he carefully checking out something new (orienting), tensed up and ready to spring into action (freezing), or in a deep state of fear (tonic immobility)? By understanding these states, we can create a more supportive environment for our horse, helping him feel secure and understood in our care.

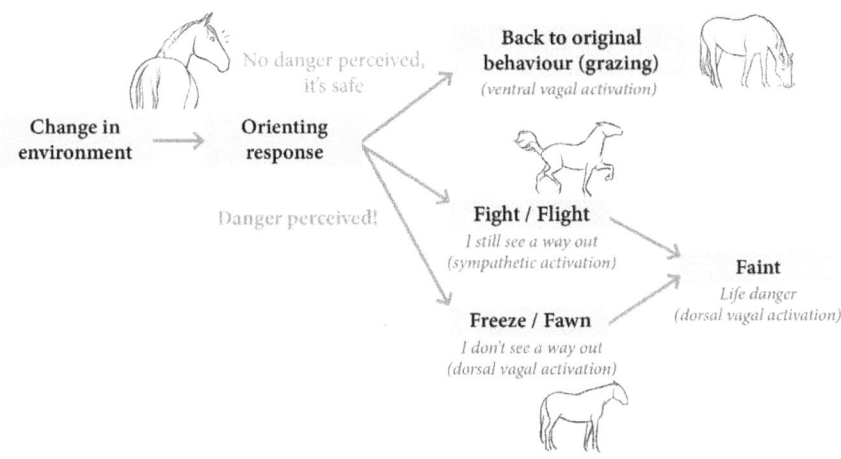

CHAPTER 18

Emotions and Trauma

When we see a horse acting out, it's easy to think he's just being overly emotional. What if I told you that what's really happening is a survival response?

First, let's be clear: emotions in horses, like in humans, are normal and healthy. They're signs of a well-functioning brain. Emotions happen within the Window of Tolerance, or the "threshold." That means they're manageable, and the horse is still able to regulate back to homeostasis.

But what happens when things escalate? Let's say a rider keeps pushing his horse too hard while ignoring repeated signs of distress (known as trigger stacking). The horse's discomfort turns into anxiety or even panic. At this point, his brain isn't operating on emotions anymore; it's reacting from a place of deep, instinctual survival.

When a horse feels threatened beyond his comfort zone, his actions are taken over by the "reptilian brain," that ancient part of the brain focused solely on survival. This triggers one of the five responses we discussed in the previous chapter: fight, flight, freeze, fawn or faint. These responses aren't emotional choices; they're automatic survival mechanisms. Unfortunately, many people, including some trainers, misinterpret these survival responses as mere emotional behavior. This misunderstanding can lead to handling methods that don't address the root cause of the horse's distress. Recognizing emotions versus survival responses in horses helps us respond to their needs more effectively.

The way we interpret and respond to a horse's behavior has profound implications for his well-being and our relationship with him. When we know the difference between emotional expressions and survival responses, we provide better care and support for our equine friends. It's a fundamental shift in perspective that has the potential to improve the lives of horses and their human companions significantly.

Recognizing unseen trauma in horses

It's upsetting when we see horses that have been clearly hurt, like those that don't get enough food or have been abused. But there's another kind of hurt in horses that's harder to see and often gets missed.

Imagine horses that just do what's being asked in a sort of robotic way. They put up with people because of previous experiences where they couldn't escape. There's no spirit in their eyes anymore. They do what they're told but they don't feel safe. Or think about horses that always seem to want more food; some people call them "greedy," but they might be acting this way because they're worried about when they'll eat again, since they've experienced real hunger when there wasn't enough food earlier in life.

And what about horses that get really upset when they're alone? Some might say they're just being over the top, but it could be because they feel scared and anxious when separated from the herd. Or maybe they've been weaned too early. These behaviors aren't random; they show us a horse that has been hurt in ways we can't always see right away.

In Chapter 3 we talked about human trauma. The above-mentioned information sheds light on a significant issue: horses can experience trauma as well, just like humans. This trauma can change how they behave in ways that might not always be obvious to us. Some may visibly act out, but others may show their trauma through subtler behavior, like turning away, an empty gaze or shallow breathing, which can be easy to overlook.

It's concerning to see how common escalating pressure, trigger stacking and even trauma is among horses, and it's even more troubling to realize some practices in the horse industry may actually contribute to this problem. Things like separating foals from their mothers too early, not taking proper care of them, moving horses from one owner to another too often, keeping horses in stalls 24/7, or using tough training methods can all cause trauma. This is especially true in high level sports, where ribbons, prestige and money make people sacrifice the welfare of their horse.

For anyone who loves horses, it's important to notice the quiet ways horses show us they're not okay because of bad experiences they've had in their lives. Once we understand what's behind these signs, we will start treating our horse friends with more kindness, respect and understanding.

I'm not talking here about the basic needs all horses should have access to, like food and water, sleep, social engagement and play with other horses, physical movement and mental stimulation. I'm talking about recognizing the subtle signals our horses are using to tell us they're not comfortable or even in pain.

Let's change the horse world into a more compassionate one. Healing goes beyond words. It's about creating an environment of safety, understanding and authenticity, allowing the horse to move past his trauma and into a state of peace and trust. We learned earlier that through neuroplasticity, the brain can rewire itself, creating new, healthier patterns. By learning about a horse's subtle signals, you can create a safe and understanding environment for him, so that every horse gets a chance to rewire his brain and have a happy life without any fear or pain.

CHAPTER 19

Building Resilience in Horses

Resilience in horses, like in humans, involves both the body and the mind. It's not just about being physically strong; it's also about having mental stability and well-being. This combination has a positive effect on health and movement, and reduces the risk of injury. Just as you regulate your own emotions, you can help your horse learn to manage his. This means recognizing when your horse is stressed and helping him return to a calm state.

The following eight steps help immensely with building up a horse's resilience:

1. Regulate yourself first

Because horses are so sensitive to your mood and emotions, the first step is to be able to regulate yourself (which you will learn how to do in more detail in Part III).

2. Reframe perspectives

Instead of thinking, "My horse is naughty," consider, "My horse doesn't understand me." The shift in perspective can change how you approach training and problem-solving.

3. Encourage state switching

Help your horse learn to transition between states of arousal and relaxation. This flexibility is a key component of resilience. Take enough breaks to give your horse time to calm down, and sometimes add a bit of extra energy or a new challenge in your training. This practice builds both physical and mental resilience.

4. Expose them to new situations

Regularly take your horse for walks in different environments. It helps him become more adaptable.

5. Encourage physical balance

A physically balanced horse is less likely to spook. While this book focuses on mental balance, remember that physical balance is equally important. Stay tuned for my next book, which will be all about helping your horse get better balanced.

6. Slow down

Sometimes, resilience is built in the quiet moments. Allow your horse to process and relax, showing him there's no rush. Slow down to catch up with your horse!

7. Embrace fun and play

Make sure to include fun activities both you and your horse enjoy. Play is a powerful tool for learning and building resilience.

8. Communicate respectfully

Instead of commanding your horse, try asking and thanking him for his cooperation. Respectful communication builds a stronger bond and mutual trust, and brings you and your horse in a heart-coherent state.

Building resilience in horses is a journey, not a destination. It requires patience, understanding, and commitment to daily practice. By focusing on both physical fitness and mental well-being, we help our horses lead happier, healthier lives. A resilient horse is a confident horse, ready to face the world with you by his side.

We are not aiming to achieve a state of perfect relaxation at all times. Life doesn't work that way, neither for us nor for our horses. Instead, we aim for a state that is functional—being able to navigate through different states as needed.

An emotionally healthy horse isn't one that's always calm. Rather, it's a horse that can move in and out of various states—calmness, alertness, and even tension—depending on what the situation demands. Life throws different scenarios at us, and sometimes, a bit of tension is exactly what's needed.

Remember, as you work with your horse, the goal is not to eliminate anxiety and tension completely; that's an unrealistic expectation. Aim for balance. This means having the flexibility to move between states with ease, and being able to recover and find relaxation again after moments of stress.

PART III

Self-regulation

This part of the book will give you short, simple, yet powerful exercises to effortlessly shift from a sympathetic, stressed state to a parasympathetic, relaxed state.

CHAPTER 20

What is Self-regulation?

At the core of self-regulation is your ability to navigate through the different states of the autonomic nervous system, finding balance and calmness within. How would you feel if you knew how to regulate yourself and go from A to B(e)?

From A	To BE
I feel tense, stressed, anxious	I feel relaxed, calm, connected
I spook when my horse spooks	I can help my horse relax
I'm frustrated	I'm curious
My horse doesn't understand me	I can communicate with my horse
My horse is doing this on purpose	I understand my horse's brain
My horse hates me	My horse seeks my presence
I'm afraid, I'm not good enough	I feel confident, I know what to do
As I grow older, I feel more afraid	I feel joy and ease with my horse
I'm the only one at my barn	I don't care what others say
I worry too much	I'm connected to my body wisdom
I need to be in control	We play based on partnership
I'm afraid to go out alone	I go on relaxed trail rides

Before I introduce you to the **ten self-regulating strategies**, let's start with a few simple steps and the different ways you can do these exercises.

So often, we rely too much on our logical brain, losing the connection with our sensitive body. We need to learn how to "drop down" from our thinking head into our feeling body. We need to reconnect to the wisdom and sensations in our body.

The exercises I've selected are quick and easy, require no special equipment or props like a yoga mat, and can all be done while standing. The beauty of these exercises is that you can do them anytime and anywhere, whether you're with your horse or standing in line at the grocery store. The steps to follow are simple:

1. Start by doing all ten strategies. Some strategies provide several exercises.

2. After trying all the exercises, select the ones that resonate with you. You can choose one exercise from each strategy or just select your favorite ones.

3. Practice these chosen exercises daily for about a week and feel what they do for your body and peace of mind.

4. From the exercises you've been practicing, select three or four that seem to bring you into a relaxed state the most or the easiest. This selection will become part of your daily routine, just like brushing your teeth. Doing them daily will create new synaptic pathways in your brain, enabling you to use these as an "emergency routine" when a stressful event or challenging situation occurs, for instance when your horse spooks.

I've listed the exercises from the head going down, as I like the idea of "dropping" from my brain into my body, but you can do them in any order you like or what feels best for you.

There are three ways to do an exercise:

1. You execute the exercise as an exercise. You read it, you do it.

2. You do the exercise mindfully, with full awareness. You are aware of your body while doing the exercise; you are aware if your muscles are tensed or relaxed; you are aware of your breathing.

3. You do the exercise as an embodied practice. You *are* the exercise—you don't have to think anymore, because your body knows the exercise. That's when you've created new synaptic pathways in your brain.

Knowledge alone is *not* enough! You need to practice in a *safe* state many times to create new neural pathways in your brain. Now when a challenging or scary situation happens, your body knows how to respond to the situation in a regulated way, because it has practiced this many times. The brain has gained an alternative to the automatic survival response based on old triggers.

My "emergency routine" is to take a deep sigh and then shake my body and jaw (often with a sound). It shifts me right back into the parasympathetic nervous system. Shifting between the different states will increase your resilience, as you will be better equipped to deal with challenging situations.

In the next chapters I will explain the ten self-regulating strategies to drop from the thinking mind into the feeling body, but for now here's a quick look at all ten. Enjoy!

0. Become the Observer

1. Check In with Yourself

2. Breathe

3. Achieve a Heart Coherent State

4. Jaw and Sound

5. Neck and Vagus Nerve

6. Shoulder Release

7. Posture

8. Spinal Alignment

9. Grounding

10. Shake Your Body!

CHAPTER 21

Step 0: Become the Observer

There is actually a step "zero," a starting point, and that is to **become the observer of yourself**. Visualize that you are hovering over yourself, like a helicopter or drone, observing your feelings, emotions and thoughts.

Often, we find ourselves reacting instinctively to situations. When we face an unexpected situation and are startled or scared, our sympathetic nervous system kicks in. As we learned in Part I, this is the part of our nervous system that controls our fight-or-flight response.

But how does it feel to be in this state? Do you make good decisions when you're stressed or scared?

Not really.

That's why it's crucial to learn how to become an observer of yourself. By observing your feelings, emotions and thoughts, you can start recognizing early signs of stress or fear. For instance, if you're walking with your horse and you sense your heart rate go up because you are anticipating a spook, that's your cue to step in and take control, for example by regulating your breath.

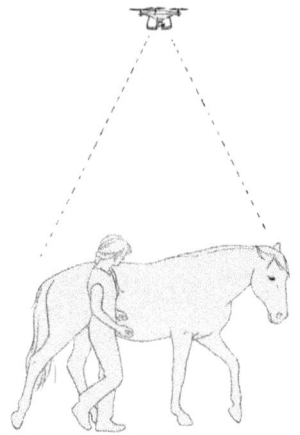 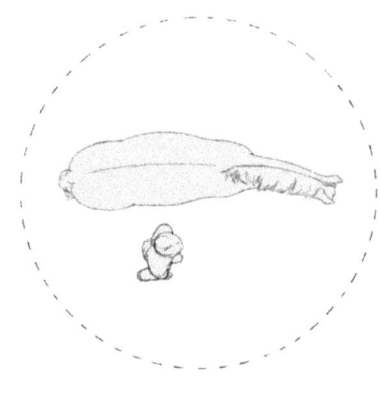

By observing all signs of your body and mind, you can intervene *before* your nervous system goes into overdrive. You can use your emergency routine to calm down and regain balance and harmony. Your ability to regulate your reactions will help you become a safe spot for your horse.

Choose the techniques that resonate with you. It's all about creating a mental image that helps you disconnect from the story or overwhelm in the moment and see the bigger picture.

Becoming an observer of yourself is not just beneficial when working with horses. It's *a skill that can transform every aspect of your life!* When you learn to become the observer of your reactions, you can avoid being sucked into stress or drama. You can take a step back, assess the situation, and make better decisions.

Remember, once you're in a state of high arousal, it becomes challenging or even virtually impossible to learn, adapt, or make sound decisions. Your nervous system is hijacked by fear and the thinking brain goes offline. Learn to observe the early signs of stress or fear, so you can intervene and regain control.

CHAPTER 22

Step 1: Check In with Yourself

Being an observer of yourself is a crucial skill. To observe effectively, you need to regularly check in with yourself. A check-in is a moment of pause, a moment where you tune into yourself and your surroundings. In this chapter I will explain in detail how you can do this.

I developed a simple check-in routine, based on a common mudra or hand gesture used in meditation, connecting your thumb and index finger. This simple gesture serves as a reminder for me to take a moment to observe and assess. Maybe this check-in routine can work for you as well.

The check-in process involves both **external** and **internal** observations. The starting position is to gently let your index finger touch your thumb on *both* hands. Now start with your left hand for the external check-in, using your senses to become more aware of your surroundings.

1. What do I see?

Move your thumb from your index finger to your middle finger and use only your eyes to take in your environment. Notice the movement of the trees, the horses around you, or any other visual cues.

2. What do I hear?

Move your thumb to your ring finger and use only your ears. Tune into the sounds around you. It could be the rustling of leaves, the sound of a tractor in the distance, or the gentle grazing of your horse.

3. What do I feel externally?

Lastly, move your thumb to your little finger and focus on the physical sensations from the outside. Feel the wind on your face, the texture of your clothes against your skin, or the earth beneath your feet.

This external check-in helps bring you into the present moment, making you more aware of your surroundings.

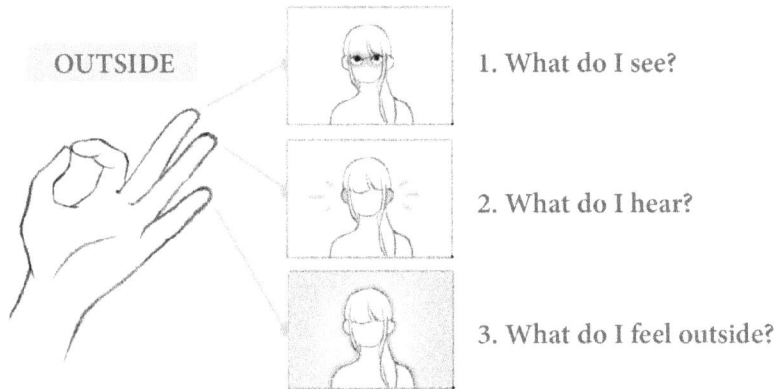

Next comes the internal check-in, using the fingers of your right hand. This involves tuning in to your physical sensations, emotions and thoughts. Your thumb and index finger of your right hand are already touching each other from the starting position.

1. What do I feel physically?

Move your thumb from your index finger to your middle finger and do a quick body scan. Be aware of any sensation like your feet on the ground, your heartbeat, or any tension in your muscles.

2. What do I feel emotionally?

Next move your thumb to your ring finger and tune in to your emotional state. Are you feeling excited, calm, anxious, happy?

3. What am I thinking?

Lastly, move your thumb to your little finger and check in with your thoughts. Are you worried about something? Are you anticipating what's next? Or perhaps you're enjoying a rare moment of quiet, with no thoughts at all.

This observing is done in a non-judgemental way, just watching and allowing the emotions to happen. The goal is not for the feelings to disappear; you're simply remaining curious about what's existing in and around your body.

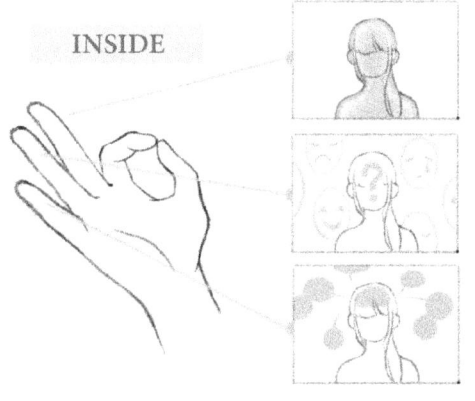

INSIDE

1. What do I feel physically?

2. What do I feel emotionally?

3. What are my thoughts?

Over time, as you practice this routine, you'll find that even the simple mudra gesture of putting your index finger and thumb together can trigger a full check-in. Your body will instinctively respond. You will automatically slow down and become present. It's like creating a *shortcut to awareness*, and nobody will notice you doing this. Even when you're walking or engaged in other activities, this simple gesture can bring you back to the present moment, allowing you to assess your state and decide how to respond.

Make checking in a habit. It's a simple task that will greatly enhance your self-awareness and ability to stay present and grounded; not just when you're with your horses, but in every aspect of your life.

CHAPTER 23

Step 2: Breathe

The way you breathe is the way you live. Full, free breathing is one of the most powerful keys to improve your physical and emotional well-being. Many of us unconsciously tighten our muscles and restrict our breathing. We learn that the less we breathe, the less we feel, and the easier it is to get through the challenges of life. Over time, this process develops habitual unconscious reactions that lock up the body. It helps prevent us from feeling stressed or hurt again. However, it also prevents our life energy from flowing freely and us from living fully.

When you become aware of your breathing and work with it consciously, you make a direct link to your autonomic nervous system. Through your breathing, it's possible to feel connected again, with yourself and with all living beings around us. Through full and conscious breathing, we can ask our horse to connect to us so we can be in the same energy bubble. From this place, the magic of true and playful togetherness can happen!

Most people breathe very shallowly. Because we breathe approximately 30,000 times per day, this is a very powerful way to increase our well-being. Best of all, breathing is free and available to us every second of every day.

103

I will explain three simple breathing techniques that will help you shift from the sympathetic to the parasympathetic state. Try them all for 3 to 5 minutes and see which one resonates with you.

Full breathing

Full breathing involves engaging three parts of your body: the belly, the ribcage, and the upper part of your chest. Visualize the air flowing into your belly as you inhale; then expand your rib cage to the sides; and lastly, fill the upper part of your lungs. Follow the path of your breath with your hands to make this connection stronger.

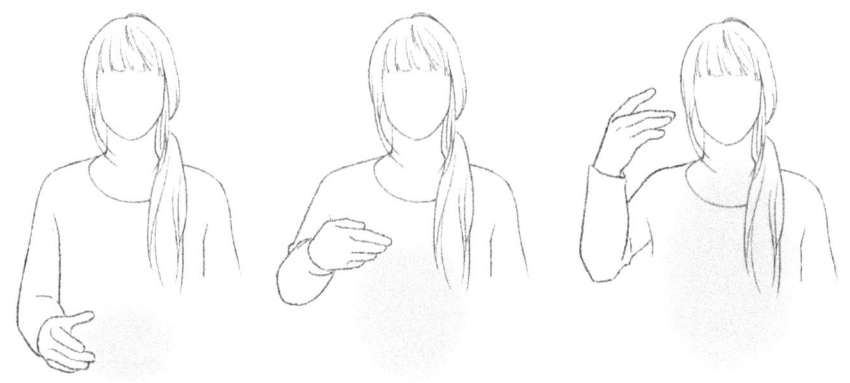

Longer exhales

The second technique involves exhaling longer than you inhale. Try breathing in for four counts (preferably using full breathing), then exhaling for six or even eight counts. Humming and singing while exhaling are also very helpful, as you will automatically breathe out longer after taking a deep breath in. And singing is fun!

Deep sigh

The third technique is the deep sigh. You've probably done this unconsciously at moments of feeling stressed or exhausted. It's a quick way to release tension and shift from a sympathetic to a parasympathetic state. You can even add a sound to it, like snorting, which our horses often do.

There is also an extra variation of the deep sigh, called the "cyclic breath." Start by taking a deep breath in. Before you exhale, take another breath in to also fill the little extensions of your lungs. Then let out a long, slow sigh, preferably with sound. People who did the cyclic breath in a breathing study group all reported significant increases in energy, joy and peacefulness, so it's worthwhile to do this on a regular basis!

Breathing practices are great to do when you're with your horse. As you calm down and become more present, your horse will respond positively, showing signs of relaxation and trust. When your horse starts to relax, he'll respond better to your cues, and you'll become more confident in your training. You're helping each other, a great method of co-regulation.

Practice breathing techniques regularly and choose the one that resonates with you the most. Remember, these breathing techniques can bring about a profound change in your life and your relationship with your horse.

CHAPTER 24

Step 3: Achieve a Heart Coherent State

Following the breathing exercises in the previous chapter, I love getting into a heart coherent state. It's a great feeling to be there and it automatically puts a smile on my face. You can find more about the concept of heart coherence at heartmath.org.

Heart coherence is a harmonious state where your heart, mind and emotions are aligned and balanced. This state promotes physical and emotional well-being, and horses love to be around you when you're in this state. Getting into a heart coherent state involves three phases:

1. Slow down your breathing.

Start counting your breathing rhythm, making sure your inhalation and exhalation are of similar length. For instance, inhale for four counts and exhale for the same. You can adjust the counts as per your comfort, but the key is to *slow down your breath*. For example, breathe in for a count of 1, 2, 3, 4, and then breathe out for a count of 1, 2, 3, 4. This slow, rhythmic breathing may even make you sigh—a sign of relaxation.

2. Focus on your heart.

Now close your eyes and bring your focus inside. Consciously shift your internal focus from your head to your heart space. You may find it helpful to place one or both hands over your heart. Continue with your slow, deep breathing. Some people find it beneficial to visualize their breath flowing in and out through their heart.

3. Radiate gratitude or love.

While maintaining your focus on your heart and your slow breathing, start radiating feelings of gratitude or love. Emotions are energy frequencies, just like radio waves, and these positive emotions have a high frequency that horses pick up and are drawn to.

Now, let's put it all together. Take a deep breath, focus on your heart, and start radiating gratitude to your horse. To induce this feeling of gratitude, look at your horse or bring a positive memory back into your mind. You might say, for example, "You're such a beautiful horse, and I love you." Watch for signs from your horse, like licking and chewing, lowering the head, or a deep sigh. These are signs that your horse is co-regulating with you.

Maintaining this heart coherent state during training can be incredibly beneficial. Continually expressing your admiration and gratitude for your horse helps sustain this state. For instance, when you ask your horse to do something, follow it up by saying "thank you" when he gives his best try.

When you're in a heart coherent state, you may notice your horse becoming more relaxed, perhaps even closing his eyes. These signs are a fantastic example of co-regulation. However, remember that it's perfectly fine if your horse gets distracted and walks away. The goal is not to force anything but to create an inviting, calm energy that your horse will want to return to.

109

CHAPTER 25

Step 4: Jaw and Sound

A lot of tension is stored in the jaw, both for horses and for humans. I learned from the Masterson Method® how to release tension in the TMJ of the horse, so I thought it would be helpful to find ways to do this for myself too.

The temporomandibular joint, or the TMJ as it's popularly known, is located just in front of your ears. To find it, place your finger there and open your mouth. You will feel your fingers sink into a newly created space. That's your TMJ area, and that's where we're going to focus on releasing tension.

The jaw drop exercise

Quite literally, you're going to let your jaw drop. This exercise may seem silly, but trust me, it's really effective. Place your fingers on your TMJ, then start making an "ph" sound while slowly exhaling. At the end of your exhale, make a "thu" sound and then let your jaw drop wide open. Repeat three or four times. Don't worry about looking funny doing it; the relaxation you'll feel in your jaw will be worth it!

The sound exercise

Next, we're going to open our mouths and make a sound at the back of our throats. You can choose any sound you like or that feels good. Personally I find "ahhh" or "uhhh" very effective. This exercise has the added benefit of activating the vagus nerve, as it's attached (among other places) to the vocal cords.

As we learned in Chapter 7, the vagus nerve is key to helping us shift from a state of stress (sympathetic) to one of relaxation (parasympathetic).

The tongue shake

Lastly there's the "tongue shake" exercise. This doesn't involve physically shaking your tongue; instead, you visualize it laying relaxed within your lower jaw. While maintaining this visualization, gently shake your head from left to right, like you're saying no.

This will automatically make your tongue "shake" a bit. You may find making a sound while doing this helpful.

The above three exercises form what I like to call the "**Jaw Release**." They're simple to do, a little bit funny to look at, but incredibly effective at releasing tension.

CHAPTER 26

Step 5: Neck and Vagus Nerve

The **vagus nerve** is a fascinating part of our anatomy, as we saw in Chapter 7. It originates in the brain and runs down our neck, acting as a communication highway between our brain and many of our major organs. We already learned that activating the vagus nerve can help us shift from a state of stress to a state of relaxation.

Every morning after I meditate, I practice some neck stretches. They're simple yet very powerful. You'll feel an instant shift when you combine the neck stretch with the eye movement.

Turning from left to right

Start by turning your head from left to right about 6 to 8 times. There's no need to rush; take it slow and feel the stretch on either side of your neck. Over time, you'll notice an increase in your neck's flexibility, which can greatly improve your posture, whether you're standing, sitting, or even riding a horse.

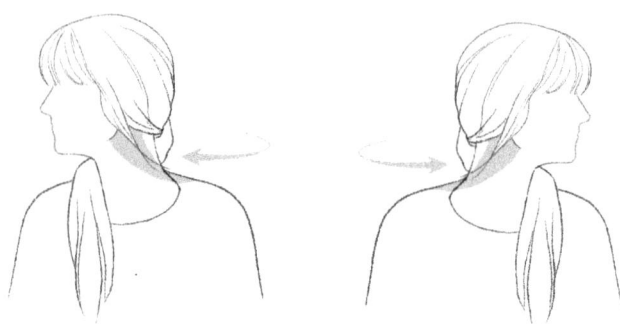

Tilting your head

The second stretch involves tilting your head towards your shoulder. However, here's a little tip: instead of thinking about bringing your ear to your shoulder (which often leads to raising your shoulder), visualize the opposite ear reaching upwards. This encourages lengthening the side of your neck rather than contracting.

Just like the previous exercise, repeat this stretch about 6 to 8 times on each side. Experiment with the speed, sometimes going a bit quicker, other times slower. For an even deeper stretch, extend your arm downwards on the side you're stretching. You'll feel a pleasant pull along your neck and shoulder. Hold the stretch for 3 to 5 seconds on each side. Find that sweet spot where the stretch feels just right without overstretching it.

Adding eye movement

For the final touch, add in eye movements. As you stretch one side, look up diagonally to the opposite side. Hold this position for about 20 seconds. You'll notice a complete stretch along your neck and might even find yourself sighing or yawning. That's a good thing! It means you've just consciously activated your vagus nerve, regulating yourself from the sympathetic state to the parasympathetic state. Then repeat the same on the other side.

115

CHAPTER 27

Step 6: Shoulder Release

We tend to store a lot of tension in our shoulders without realizing it. By doing shoulder exercises, you can literally drop some heavy weight that you might be carrying around.

Shoulder roll

The first is a classic one, the shoulder roll. It's easy to do and feels wonderful. Start by rolling your shoulders backwards while your arms hang loosely by your sides. Do this about 5 or 6 times, taking care to really feel the movement in your shoulders. Then change the direction and roll your shoulders forward. This simple movement can work wonders in releasing tension in your shoulders. It's like giving your shoulders a mini-massage!

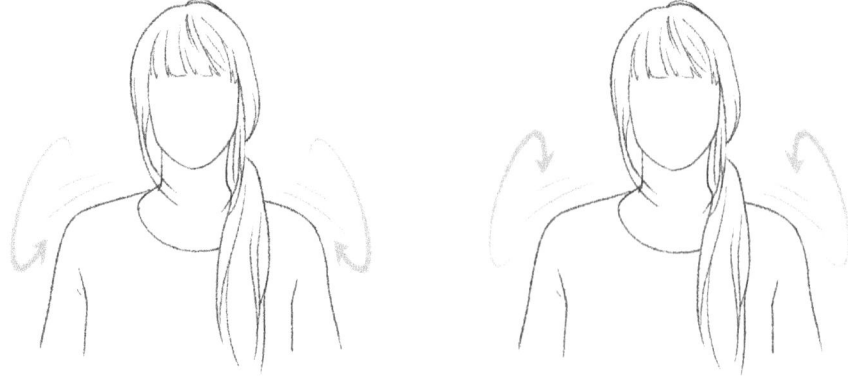

Shoulder drop

Next, we move on to the shoulder lift and drop. Lift your shoulders as high as you can, almost as if you're trying to touch your ears with your shoulders. Hold this position for a moment, allowing yourself to feel the tension. Then, with a big sigh or other sound, let your shoulders drop. It's like you're tricking your body into creating tension, only to release it immediately. This sudden release is like letting go of a heavy weight you've been carrying around. Do this 2–3 times.

Add cyclic breath

Now, let's take things up a notch. Combine the shoulder drop with the cyclic breath you learned earlier. As you lift your shoulders, inhale deeply, with the extra inhale at the end. Then as you drop your shoulders, exhale with a loud sigh. This combination of movement and breath can provide a deep sense of relaxation.

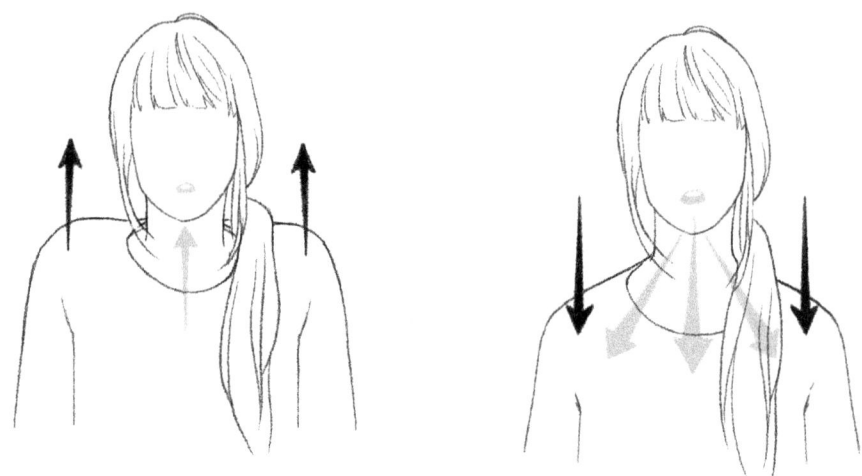

I like to add a little body shake at the end, after dropping the shoulders. It's like shaking off any residual tension or stress.

The above exercises form what I call the "**Shoulder Release**." They're easy to do, require no special equipment, and can be done anywhere, anytime.

CHAPTER 28

Step 7: Posture

Our posture is a powerful communicator. It's like our body's signature. It tells a story about what we're feeling inside. When we're scared or anxious, we contract and close ourselves off. Our shoulders hunch, our heads drop, and we make ourselves small. Conversely, when we're feeling confident and in control, our posture is open and expansive.

But have you ever thought about it the other way around? Just as your emotions influence your posture, your posture can also influence your emotions. Take a moment to try this little experiment: walk around in a tight and contracted posture. How does that make you feel? Then switch to a more open and upright posture. You'll quickly realize that just changing your physical stance can significantly alter your emotional state.

However, an overly dominant or assertive posture isn't the solution either. Although it might give you a sense of power, it often results in losing the connection with those around you, including your horse. Did you know that each posture also has its own thoughts and words? Walking in a closed and contracted posture usually brings up thoughts like "I'm nobody. I'm not good enough." Making your posture big and overpowering comes with thoughts like "I need to be the boss. I need to be in control."

The habitual posture we have often originates from early childhood experiences, and is a result of the early wiring of the nervous system we explained in Chapter 2 of this book. When we can walk around in an open and present state, the words and thoughts that go with that include "I'm curious. I'm interested. Who are you? How can we connect?"

I believe we all would like to be "present." Being present means being *grounded*, *aware* and *connected*. It involves walking around with an open posture, breathing deeply, and being mindful of your surroundings. It's about tuning in to your inner self and understanding the state of your horse. This presence brings you into a ventral vagal state, which is associated with feelings of safety and social engagement.

I learned a simple trick about posture after my spinal injury. I open my hands while walking, facing the palms of my hands forward. This greatly improves and opens my posture, and it is done by simply turning the thumbs outward. This small gesture instantly opens up my chest, allowing me to breathe more deeply and maintain an open, present posture. It has been a game changer as far as being present.

So, start by observing your normal state. Are you generally making yourself small, or do you tend to overcompensate with a stiff and erect posture? Once you've identified your habitual posture, practice being present whenever you remind yourself of it. When you're grounded and present, you can connect with yourself, and from that place you can truly connect with your horse.

CHAPTER 29

Step 8: Spinal Alignment

The exercise in the previous chapter on posture sets the stage for understanding spinal alignment. You can think of your body as divided into three parts:

- the head and neck
- the chest and arms
- the pelvis and legs

Start by observing yourself. Is your head generally leaning forward or backward? Can you find the middle? Do the same observation with the central part of your body. Are your chest and arms forward? Or are they slightly behind the rest of your body? Repeat this observation for the lower part of your body. Is your pelvis tilted forward or backward? Are your knees locked backward or do they point forward?

To find your spinal alignment, you need to "stack" these three parts on top of each other. Start from the ground up: make sure your feet are grounded, your knees aren't locked, and your pelvis is above your feet. Then place your rib cage over your pelvis and, finally, position your head on top of your spine in a balanced way, without tilting forward or backward. This exercise helps you focus on your spinal alignment and center line, to find a centered state of being. By bringing awareness to it, you can change your posture consciously instead of being stuck in your unconscious habit.

A helpful practice to maintain spinal alignment is swaying. Visualize yourself as a vertical line, like having a vertical kebab running through the center of your body, and sway around it. This simple exercise teaches you to stay centered and maintain your vertical alignment. It's not just relaxing but also helps to really improve an aligned riding posture.

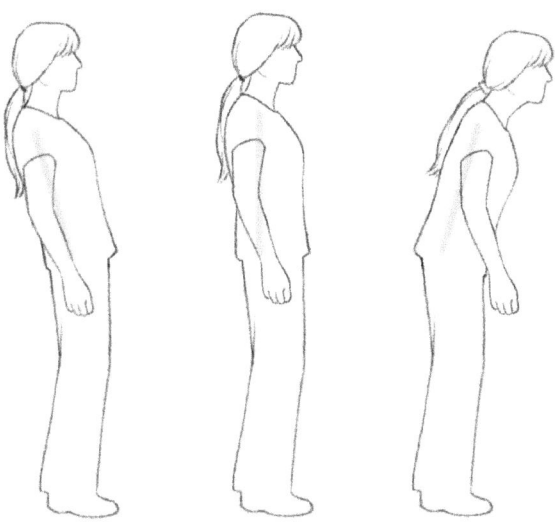

CHAPTER 30

Step 9: Grounding

Grounding, as the name suggests, is about connecting with the ground beneath you. It's about feeling your feet strongly planted on the earth and letting that sensation anchor you. It's another simple yet powerful practice that can make you feel more confident, calm and present.

When I focus on my feet while grounding, I immediately feel a heaviness. It's as if I suddenly become more aware of my feet's relationship with gravity, and they often start to tingle. I often wonder, was this sensation always there and I just wasn't aware of it? Or did it appear because I focused on it? Either way, it's an interesting phenomenon that helps bring me to the present moment.

To help you get started with grounding, I want to share three visualization techniques I often use:

1. Growing roots

Close your eyes and imagine yourself as a tree, with roots growing from your feet and going deep into the earth. This visualization makes me feel so sturdy that it feels like no one could push me over.

2. Standing by the seashore

Visualize standing at the beach, with waves washing over your feet. As the water recedes, feel how it sucks you deeper into the sand, making you feel more grounded.

3. Magnets

Picture magnets on the ground and on the soles of your feet. Feel the magnetic pull, keeping your feet firmly planted on the ground.

Once you've practiced grounding while standing still, it's time to bring it into movement. Can you walk in a grounded way? You'll notice that this practice slows you down and makes you more conscious of your steps.

When I'm walking with a horse that's feeling anxious, grounding immediately helps me stay calm and centered. I focus on my feet, feeling the magnets or visualizing the roots. With every step, I feel more connected to the ground. This sense of stability and presence tends to rub off on the horse, making him less spooky.

CHAPTER 31

Step 10: Shake Your Body!

Finally, I want to share one of my absolute favorites—shaking. When I was teaching "down under" in Australia, people who joined the clinic even named this exercise after me, calling it the "Lucie Shake." It's a fun technique that helps release tension and feels very liberating!

Tension and emotions are stored in our body. Animals know how to "shake it off" after they've encountered a threat or challenging situation. However, we humans pretend all is well and keep the accumulated aroused energy stored in our body.

First, try this little experiment. Shake your hand loosely for a moment and then make one finger stiff and shake your hand again. You'll notice that the rest of your hand can't shake anymore. This shows that tension in one part of your body affects other parts of your body.

The concept of tense body parts blocking movement is crucial when riding. If you have tension in your right foot, for instance, it can create tension in other parts of your body. This makes it harder to move freely and follow the movement of your horse. Sometimes we're not even aware we're carrying tension. That's when "shaking it off" comes in handy!

Shaking is a fantastic way to release tension. You can slowly build it up, starting to shake one part of your body, then extend it to other parts until you eventually do a full body shake. You can start, for instance, by shaking your hand.

Then your wrist.

Followed by your elbow.

And finally, your shoulder.

Do this for about 20 seconds, then have a short break and let your arm hang down.

You may find that the arm you've been shaking feels a bit longer than before. It sometimes really is! That's because shaking has helped release tension, relax muscles, and increase range of motion.

You can start with any part of your body. I usually begin with my wrists, then my elbows, and then my shoulders. Once I've shaken these parts, I start bouncing lightly on my feet, letting

127

the shaking motion travel through my body. I also shake my jaw and make some sounds to release tension in my face. I love this exercise; it's part of my emergency routine!

The beauty of shaking is that you can do it anywhere, anytime. I've done it in public places; and yes, people have given me funny looks. But guess what?

I don't care anymore, and neither should you.

It's far more important to get into a self-regulated state than to worry about what others might think. Dare to be present. Just shake it off and see how it works for you.

CHAPTER 32

Resilience: Creating New Pathways in Your Brain

We've come to the final chapter of our self-regulation journey—resilience. This capability is crucial in our daily lives and when working with horses. I touched upon resilience in Chapter 12 and will now add a few practical tips.

Resilience is about being able to shift from one state to another effortlessly. In the context of our self-regulation journey, it's about moving from a sympathetic state (fight or flight) back to a parasympathetic state (rest and digest) or ventral vagal state (social engagement system).

Remember the ten-step self-regulating routine we discussed? Now, pick your favorite three or four strategies and make them into an "emergency routine" you do every day. For me, grounding, a deep sigh, shaking, and making a sound are part of my emergency routine. When my horse spooks, I immediately turn to these techniques so I don't spook with him. Instead, I radiate to my horse that I'm grounded and present and there's nothing to worry about.

How can you build resilience in your daily life? The key is to practice consciously shifting between states.You need to experience the sympathetic state—an increased heart rate, heightened alertness—and then consciously shift back to a relaxed state.

Try running a short stretch or doing jumping jacks, anything physical that increases your heart rate. After a short burst of activity, stand still, ground yourself, breathe deeply, and apply any other exercises from your emergency routine. Repeat this cycle to exercise your ability to shift states.

Taking cold showers is another great way to practice this. The cold triggers a sympathetic response. Can you breathe and regulate yourself under the cold water? This technique aligns with Wim Hof's "cold exposure" method, and there are lots of scientific reports showing various health benefits of cold exposure.

Besides physical resilience, building mental resilience is equally important. This involves facing things you find scary while staying in contact with yourself and, if necessary, regulating yourself. For instance, if you find it daunting to be in large crowds, consciously put yourself in that situation. Observe where you are and how you feel. Check your environment and yourself. Then, consciously regulate yourself.

Remember, always *keep it safe*. Stretch yourself just a little bit, then retreat to safety.

One fun (and a bit challenging) exercise I once did is just standing still on a busy shopping street and focusing on a certain point. Despite people staring at me or starting to talk to me, I would practice grounding, adjusting my posture, opening my chest, and other self-regulation techniques. It taught me to regulate myself in challenging situations.

Creating new neural pathways

Our brain is a remarkable organ; it has the ability to change and adapt, a concept known as neuroplasticity (as we discussed in Chapter 11). When we practice observing and regulating ourselves in daily situations, it helps to rewire our nervous system. Each time we practice our self-regulation techniques, we're essentially creating new neural pathways. These pathways become stronger and more efficient with repetition.

When you encounter a spooky situation while riding your horse, instead of panicking or tensing up, you'll have a new option. You can now use the techniques you learned in this book. Because you've practiced them many times in safe situations, your body remembers to regulate yourself. This isn't just theory; it's backed by neuroscience.

Remember, this journey is all about practice, practice, practice. So, play around with these techniques, experiment with them, and make them your own. The more you practice, the better you'll get at regulating yourself in all kinds of situations.

You now have techniques to regulate yourself, helping you to become a nervous system navigator. In the next part we'll explore how we can help our horses to feel safe and relaxed as well.

PART IV

Co-regulation

This part will explain the key principles of co-regulation. When you know how to help your horse relax and feel safe in your presence, he will look to you when his brain perceives danger.

CHAPTER 33

The Play Safe Principles

In the previous part of this book, you learned ten strategies for self-regulation. In this last part, the key principles of co-regulation will be explained. When you know how to help your horse relax and feel safe in your presence, he will look to you for answers in situations when his brain perceives danger.

Co-regulation lies at the heart of all human relationships. According to Polyvagal Theory, *it is the reciprocal sending and receiving of signals of safety*. It's not just the absence of danger; instead, it's the connection between two nervous systems, each nourishing and regulating the other in the process. It's when someone feeling relaxed and regulated "shares their calm" with someone else experiencing stressful emotions. It's a warm, responsive and empathetic way to support another being and regulate their nervous system as they work through perceived negative feelings. It's a mutual exchange of energy and presence, fostering connection on a deeper level. This process can take place between all mammals, also from human to horse and from horse to human.

Horses as co-regulators

Horses are natural co-regulators. They are incredibly sensitive to human emotions and states, picking up our energy and responding to our hidden intentions. A horse's presence becomes a mirror, reflecting the authenticity of our internal experiences, inviting us to be present and attuned in the moment.

We are all energy beings. All hearts have an electromagnetic field. According to a study by HearthMath Institute, a human heart radiates an energy field up to eight to ten feet (around three meters), as measured by a magnetometer. A horse's electromagnetic field is stronger and about five times larger, creating a sphere-shaped field completely surrounding you when you're near a horse. The energy field of a horse can influence your heart rhythm and emotions.

There are many equine-assisted coaching and therapy methods in which horses help humans. In this part of the book, we want to reverse it and look at it from the other side. How can *we* recognize the state of our horse and help him feel safe and connected?

Humans as co-regulators

Being effective co-regulators involves attuning to the state of the horse's nervous system and creating an environment where the horse feels safe to express himself. It's about becoming a steady presence, offering calm energy, and intuitively responding to the horse's emotional shifts. In this interaction, the human becomes a companion and guide in the journey of regulation.

How can we help our horse relax, even in challenging situations? By becoming a *trustworthy human!*

There are eight principal steps needed to achieve this. To guide you through these steps and help you remember them, I call them the **Play Safe Principles** (PSP). Each letter of P.L.A.Y. S.A.F.E. stands for one principle, and each is explained more fully as the book continues. Since most of these principles are still to come in Part IV, let me list them all here:

P: Polyvagal principles

Understand Polyvagal Theory and learn how the polyvagal principles can be translated and integrated into your horse training. Know the meaning of neuroception, the orienting response, and the Window of Tolerance.

L: Listen to your horse

Observe your horse without any goals, judgment or interpretations. Recognize the different states of the autonomic nervous system — safety, activation, shutdown — and where your horse feels safe. Everything is information; train your eye to see the subtle details.

A: Allow! The power of pause

Allow! Take a step back and embrace the power of pause to create moments of stillness and reflection. These pauses give your horse the time he needs to process information and regulate his emotions. Take moments of stillness to allow your horse to self-regulate and return to a state of relaxation and connection.

Y: "Yes" only has meaning when "No" is an option

Grant your horse the freedom to choose. Create an environment where saying "no" carries no adverse consequences. Working at liberty and offering your horse the freedom to choose is a gift you give with an open heart. By allowing him to walk away, we honor his autonomy and strengthen his trust. In the flow of freedom, your connection deepens, grounded in mutual respect and understanding.

S: Self-regulation

Become a beacon of safety for your horse by being present, grounded and relaxed. Radiate care and compassion from a heart coherent place, and become a person your horse loves to be with. To radiate gratitude, care and compassion, you need to feel good about yourself!

A: Attune to your horse's needs (co-regulation)

What does your horse need? It could be gentle activation, or soft touch to help him find relaxation. In your presence, let your horse discover various ways of connection and companionship.

F: Fun!

Introduce play and curiosity. Add new objects to your horse's environment and let him explore. Play builds relationships and induces positive feelings, which contribute to a shared well-being.

E: Explore new situations

Increase resilience by gently exposing your horse to new situations. A foundation of trust and co-regulation will enable you to guide your horse through unfamiliar terrain, along flapping plastic, or other strange objects you encounter when working with your horse or going for trail rides. You now know that together, you can navigate any challenge coming your way.

CHAPTER 34

Co-dysregulation

We can help our horses feel safe when we've learned to self-regulate. However, it also works the other way around. Because we're all energy beings, we unconsciously influence all the beings around us. Have you ever entered a room where people have been fighting or arguing? Even if the people aren't there anymore, you can still feel the tension in the room.

Horses are even more receptive to energy than humans, so they can experience co-dysregulation in the presence of a person experiencing emotional distress. When you experience frustration or anger, they often choose to move away from this source of discomfort if allowed to do so.

Co-(dys)regulation among horses is known as group or herd dynamics. If one horse is overexcited or fearful, it affects all other members of the herd. This makes sense. If a horse, being part of a herd, signals danger, it wouldn't be smart to wait until each individual herd member sees the threat. At that point, it could be too late. So, when one horse starts to run, the rest of the herd joins instantly and they all run away together.

This explains the importance of self-regulation, as we discussed in a previous part of this book. When you feel frustrated or angry, or you're going through an emotional period, don't bring this to your horse. Practice self-awareness and maintain a balanced and calm presence around him. Take a step back, check in with yourself, breathe, shake it off, or use any other technique to regulate your own nervous system, so you can be a soothing influence for your equine partner.

CHAPTER 35

Signals of Stress

Before we discuss various co-regulating techniques, we need to recognize the signals of stress. Do you recognize the subtle signals when your horse feels stressed? Are you really listening to your horse? Horses are perfectly capable of self-regulation. Do you give your horse time to do so? As demonstrated in the research of Rachael Draaisma, when a horse is trying to self-regulate, they display visible calming signals. Do you recognize all these calming signals, or are you missing some of them?

It's human nature to "turn up the volume" if our horse isn't responding the way we want it to. When we ask again, adding more pressure, we're choosing submission over partnership. It may be the hardest thing of all to step back and really listen! What is your horse trying to tell you? How do you "label" your horses' behavior?

- When your horse is slow, do you call this "lazy" or "apprehensive?"
- When your horse is yawning, do you perceive this as "boredom?" Or could your horse be self-regulating?
- When your horse looks away, do you label that as "disrespect" or "disobedience," or is it being distracted by possible danger?

If we want to help our horse through co-regulation, we first need to recognize the initial signals when our horse is ramping up into the sympathetic arousal state. Just like humans, every horse has its unique way of expressing stress. These signals can vary based on their upbringing, previous experiences, and environment.

We all recognize a stressful horse when it's running around snorting, with the head and tail up high. Other horses show repetitive behavior like pacing back and forth, cribbing or weaving. These horses are already in a state of being overwhelmed. It will take time for them to find relaxation again. However, as you start noticing the initial signals of stress, you can give them time to self-regulate or help them with co-regulation techniques. Let's examine the subtle signals of a horse progressing into a state of arousal:

Eyes

Have you ever heard the saying, "Eyes are the windows to the soul?" This is especially true for horses. When a horse is relaxed, its eyes will be almond-shaped. But when alert, you'll notice a slight frown, the front of the eyes lifting up a bit. Some horses stop blinking when they feel stressed, so that's another sign to look for.

Ears

When a horse's ears are pricked forward, it means the horse is alert to potential danger (known as the orienting response, as we've discussed in detail previously). When you're training your horse, you might notice that the inside ear often points towards you, indicating that the horse is listening, while the outside ear casually sweeps around. However, if both ears suddenly point in one direction or move quickly in all directions, it could signify alertness or even tension.

Nose

When you see wrinkles above the nose, or wide-open nostrils, this can indicate stress.

Mouth

A stressed horse often shows a tight mouth or a tight lower lip with subtle wrinkles. Some horses even fidget with their tongue or start to bite things when they're feeling anxious.

Jaw

When a horse is chewing, you can see a large muscle on the jaw, the masseter muscle. When a horse is tense, he may clench his teeth, causing tension in the jaw and TMJ. You can see lines appearing on the jaw where this muscle tightens.

Tail

A stressed horse will have a tail that is clamped down. There is no natural swinging of the tail in movement.

Position of the head

Ideally, when you're working with your horse, its head should be at the level of the chest. If the head is lifted up, even slightly, it can mean there is tension. This can also cause tension in the horse's back.

Horse looking away

Some people might interpret a horse looking away as being disrespectful. In reality, it could mean one of two things: the horse is *distracted by something* in its environment; or the horse is *feeling too much pressure* from you.

Head movement

Stress or tension can also be observed in the horse's head movement. If the horse's head bobs more upward, it's a sign the horse is pushing more, which can create tension in his back. On the other hand, if the head movement tends downward, it indicates a relaxed posture.

Fidgeting

Fidgeting is any kind of restlessness, such as your horse starting to move around, biting the lead rope or your jacket, scratching himself, or similar behavior.

Remember, these signals are your horse's way of asking, *"Am I still safe?"* Instead of interpreting these as signs of disobedience or disrespect, we should reassure them that they are safe. By doing this, we build trust with our horses.

Recognizing and understanding these signals is a bit like learning a new language—namely, the language of horses. And just like any language, it takes time and practice to become fluent. Once you do, you'll be able to communicate more effectively with your horse, build a stronger relationship with them, and enable more effective co-regulation.

CHAPTER 36

Signals of Release

In the previous chapter, we looked at how to recognize when a horse is stressed. Horses also send out signals as they start to relax. It's helpful to know and recognize these signals too.

When I learned the **Masterson Method**® more than ten years ago, I started to recognize the subtle signals horses were showing to release tension. It completely changed my way of training. As I became more aware of what my horse was trying to tell me, I started to give him more frequent breaks. Although a lot of the signals are universal, every horse has its own preferred way of releasing. Once you start paying attention, you'll find the subtle details of calming signals and release patterns in your horse.

Let us look at the subtle signals of a horse progressing into a state of relaxation:

Eyes

When a horse starts to relax, his eyes will soften in an almond-shaped way. They might even start to half-close. It's as if they're looking at the world through a soft-focus lens.

Ears

You might also see a change in the ears. When your horse starts to be more at ease, the ears become floppy, like a pair of relaxed rabbit ears.

Nose

The wrinkles around the nostrils will disappear. Sometimes little drops of fluid start dripping from the nose.

Mouth

The lips are loose with no tension or stress lines. Sometimes the lower lip really hangs down, showing a gap between the lower and upper lip.

Jaw

A relaxed jaw has no tension lines in the masseter muscle. The teeth are not clenched together and you can see movement in the TMJ.

Tail

When a horse is relaxed, his tail will be loose and swing freely in movement.

Position of the head

A horse starting to relax will lower his head to chest level or even lower.

Head movement

Another sign of relaxation is the movement of the horse's head. Instead of bobbing upwards, it will start to bob downwards, almost like he's nodding in agreement with you.

Besides the above mentioned signs of relaxation, there are some bigger common signals of releasing tension:

Licking and chewing

Some people think that licking and chewing means the horse is overly stressed, but that's not necessarily true. When a horse is active, his digestion system slows down. But when a horse starts to relax, the digestion system is activated again, producing saliva. This is what causes the horse to start licking and chewing.

Yawning

When some people see a horse yawn, they say "he's bored" or "he can't handle the work anymore." However, similar to people, yawning often is a big release of tension in the jaw and the rest of the body, shifting from a sympathetic state to a state of relaxation.

Deep sigh

Like humans, horses can take a deep sigh. It's as if the horse is letting go of all his worries with one deep breath. You might notice a change in their breathing pattern right before this happens. Often the breathing will speed up a bit before slowing down, culminating in a deep sigh.

Horses are individuals, each with their unique ways of expressing themselves. Getting to know them and recognizing their subtle signals for stress and self-regulation gives us the opportunity to provide the best care for them. For example, some horses might find it difficult to stand still for long periods. They might start fidgeting or nibbling at things. Taking them for a little walk will often help. For horses like that, movement releases tension, just like taking a short walk can help you clear your head when you're feeling stressed.

Other horses can stand still for hours without showing any signs of stress. That's why it's so important to get to know your horse and understand his specific signals.

Remember when we talked about fidgeting in the previous chapter? It might seem an odd behavior, but it's actually quite important. Your horse could be saying, *"I'm about to let go of my stress, but I'm not quite ready yet."* It's similar to you trying to solve a tricky puzzle. You're on the verge of figuring it out and tapping your foot or twirling your hair without even realizing it. So don't punish him for fidgeting, just help him relax by giving him time.

Here's a summary of the most common release signals:

- Facial expression is relaxed
- Soft eyes (almond shape)
- Blinking
- Lowering the head
- Downward "bobbing" of the head (in movement)
- Soft nostrils (no wrinkles)
- Loose lower lip
- Smooth jaw (no lines)
- Floppy ears

- Licking and chewing (digestion system is activated)
- Sounds in the stomach (digestion system is activated)
- Yawning
- Snorting
- Relaxed tail
- Shaking of head or whole body
- Shifting weight
- Nose or eyes start dripping

All these signals indicate that the horse is releasing stress. It's their way of self-regulating. After releasing tension, the horse feels present again and often seeks connection (or in other words, they enter the ventral vagal state). We can help them by staying calm and relaxed too. Then, from this place, we can help them with co-regulating techniques.

CHAPTER 37

What Does My Horse Need?

In the previous chapters we talked about recognizing your horse's subtle signals of stress as well as the signals of release. But what if your horse doesn't show any signals at all? What if your horse is just standing there, not moving? Is your horse resting, or is it in a dorsal vagal shutdown mode?

This is why it's so important to recognize the state of the nervous system your horse is in. What your horse needs depends on their state of stress. Remember, though, the first priority is always to make them feel *safe*! That's why we need to observe our horses, not only with our eyes but also on an energetic level.

When we really tune in to our horse, we're able to feel the difference between a relaxed horse and a shutdown horse. A relaxed horse shows signals like we discussed in the previous chapter—floppy ears, almond-shaped or half-closed eyes, blinking every now and then, maybe a cocked leg. A shutdown horse often has a staring gaze and hardly blinks. It looks like a statue—the body of the horse is still there, but the spirit is gone. My heart aches when I see a horse that needs to dissociate from his body to survive in our human world.

If a horse is in shutdown mode, they don't respond to external input anymore. They have literally disconnected from their surroundings. People sometimes think their horse is calm because he doesn't respond to a waving flag, but maybe the horse is not calm at all. Maybe the horse knows it can't escape from the flag and has shut down. This process of exposing a horse to a certain stimulus until he doesn't respond anymore is called flooding. We don't want to go there!

When you feel a horse is in shutdown mode, the first thing to do is to make him feel safe, and then add gentle activation to encourage him to be present again. The best way to do this is to take him outside with other calm horses in a safe environment, where he can freely move around. You might sit in the field with him and just radiate that you're a safe spot as well, being part of his little herd. Then you can take the horse for a walk on a halter. Go to different spots where you let the horse graze. Encourage movement, because that will bring him out of shutdown mode. Remember to make it easy for him. The goal is not to force movement, but instead gently encourage it, so he can start to feel his body again.

If your horse is moving towards the sympathetic state or the fight-or-flight response, which is more common during training, the approach will be slightly different. The priority is still that the horse feels safe again; however, the focus now is not on activation but on relaxation.

When I notice the first signals of stress, I combine the following two steps:

1. I check in with myself and self-regulate, as we discussed in Part III. I usually automatically do my emergency routine of grounding, shaking and making a sound.

2. I pause and step back! I allow the horse to self-regulate by taking a break (more on this in the next chapter). I give him space to assess the situation (i.e. orienting response) to see if there is possible danger (through neuroception).

That will give me time to evaluate what is needed. This depends on the situation, the horse, and my goals for this session. The desired state is different when I want to do a bodywork session (i.e. achieve a dorsal vagal state), go for a nice walk together (ventral vagal) or work on a collected canter (sympathetic).

However, if a horse starts running in a highly stressful state, I try to intervene. Prolonged running can trigger the sympathetic nervous system and push him further into the fight-or-flight response, so I'll try to block his path to stop him from running.

To summarize as a general "rule" for the question "what does my horse need?"...

If in shutdown mode (i.e. dorsal vagal state), the goal is to encourage your horse from immobilization to gentle activation. Go for a walk, entice curiosity, and make it easy to move.

If in a state of stress (fight-or-flight state), the goal is relaxation. Start with self-regulation, make the distance bigger, and give him an opportunity to self-regulate and express himself. Then see if you can help him even more with co-regulating techniques.

If your horse goes into real fear-based running, try to interrupt this pattern, as this flight state triggers even more sympathetic arousal.

I have created a five-step pre-training plan that will help you optimize your training session:

1. Think of your goal for this training
2. Recognize the present state of the ANS of yourself and your horse
3. Determine the desired state for both
4. Use your favorite self-regulation exercises to get in the desired state
5. Help your horse with co-regulation tools to the desired state

You can use the link at the beginning of this book to download this plan in worksheet form.

Make self-regulation the new way of being with your horse and give your horse the opportunity to self-regulate as well. Breathe, ground, drop your energy, shake away your own tension and become a safe place—the human your horse wants to be with.

CHAPTER 38

Allow! The Power of Pause

This chapter is about allowing! Allow time, allow self-regulating, allow processing time.

During my training, I give my horse a lot of breaks. I've come to recognize the "power of pause" as a simple yet powerful tool that provides optimal learning conditions. Learning only takes place in the safe zone, so giving breaks is essential to creating the best learning conditions for your horse.

We've discussed the three states of the autonomic nervous system—sympathetic (activation when feeling safe, fight or flight when unsafe), ventral vagal (relaxed and social), and dorsal vagal (rest and digest when feeling safe, shutdown when unsafe). We already know that learning only takes place in the *green zone* of the ventral vagal state, as well as the sympathetic state or dorsal vagal state with the **ventral brake still active**. If during training your horse shows signs of moving toward the sympathetic state, giving him a break will help shift him back into the green zone.

If you ignore the signals and continue with the training, asking your horse for more and more, it's called "trigger stacking." You then risk pushing him into the *red zone* or the fight-or-flight state. In this state, the horse's only focus is **survival**.

156

He's not in a position to learn anything new. His sole aim is to escape the stressful situation.

That's why keeping your horse in the green zone during training is so crucial. Here, they are relaxed, attentive and ready to learn. Your horse may shift a little towards the sympathetic state during training. That's okay. We need some energy and arousal to perform a canter pirouette; however, the key is to always bring him back to the green zone by giving him breaks.

As mentioned before, it's not just the break and release that teaches. It's the pause afterwards that facilitates learning. During these breaks, your horse gets a chance to process and store the new information, and create new neural pathways in their brain. This is when consolidation and learning take place (for more, review Chapter 14 on how horses learn).

If you train your horse for an hour without any breaks, he might not remember anything the next day. But if you break down the training into smaller segments with regular breaks in between, your horse will find it easier to absorb and retain new information.

The frequency of breaks can vary depending on what you're teaching. If it's something new, your horse might get confused more easily. So, you'll need to give him more breaks to build new neural pathways. If it's something he already knows, you can ask for a bit more or a bit longer to increase endurance before giving him a break. To summarize: during your training, explain something to your horse in little steps. Give many breaks, especially when you're teaching something new!

Allowing time is a magical tool when exploring new surroundings as well. For example, during a trail ride with one of my horses, a big truck was parked on the side of the road. My horse stopped when he first noticed the truck. Some people might say I should stay on and push my horse forward to "show him who's the boss" and to "not let my horse win." But horses don't understand the concept of "winning." They only want to be safe.

So I waited, giving my horse time to assess the situation and to regulate himself. I made sure I regulated myself as well, so I breathed deeply and radiated to him that it was safe. Then I waited for a signal that he was shifting from the sympathetic nervous system to the parasympathetic nervous system. I watched for his body to go back to "neutral," with a deep sigh, a dropping of the head, or licking and chewing. Then I knew my horse was ready to listen to me again, so I could invite him to move forward...at least until he decided to stop again. Then I repeated the process until my horse was ready to pass this obstacle. This can happen on trail rides!

For me, the general rule with scary things is to give my horse time. Don't push them. Never go over the threshold where your horse will disconnect and is not able to listen to any of your guidance anymore.

CHAPTER 39

YES Only Has Meaning When NO Is an Option

When I meet a new horse, I prefer to start at liberty in a big enough space, like an arena or a big paddock, where the horse can freely walk around. I prefer this instead of a round pen, because in a round pen the horse doesn't have an honest opportunity to move away from me. Liberty training is not your horse sticking with you all the time. It's about *giving horses the freedom to express themselves and giving them a choice.*

I believe a "yes" only has meaning when "no" is also an option. I want to train my horse where it's also fun for him. As people say in Italian, "*Con su permesso,*" meaning "with your permission." The beauty of liberty training is that it gives me a wealth of information about my horse that I may not get when I have him on a line, even a loose one. The ability to express himself freely can be incredibly revealing.

How do I start? Because I believe liberty training is such an integral part of my Play Safe principles, I'll give you some steps I use to introduce liberty training, in particular when I introduce myself to a new horse. First, I step into the space where the horse is and just walk around. I have no obvious focus on the horse. I just watch him from the corner of my eye.

Next, I walk up to the horse, extending my arm with the back of my hand upwards, as if it's the nose of another horse. If the horse sniffs my hand, I walk away. If the horse doesn't respond, I use some self-regulating practices, like breathing, a deep sigh and grounding. If the horse still doesn't show any interest in my hand, I walk away again.

After that, I follow my intuition, depending on the reaction of the horse. I might approach from another side. If the horse starts walking and is okay with me close by, I may walk with the horse. If the horse is just standing in a corner, I may invite the horse to move and ask for gentle activation. I always make sure the horse is seeing what I'm doing and I never move unexpectedly. Remember, this is not liberty training, this is introducing yourself to the horse, and gaining his trust using a liberty approach.

What are the advantages of starting at liberty?

Information

I gather information and observe any early signals of stress. Everything the horse does gives me valuable information. What state of the nervous system is he in? Does he prefer going left or right? Is he curious? Does he seek my company?

Honest opinion

On a lunge or leadrope, a horse often complies because he knows he doesn't have a choice. What happens when I take the rope away? I get an honest opinion from my horse. This allows me to think about how to become the human my horse wants to be with. When he chooses to interact with me, it's by choice. Now I can ask for movement and start training without any stress.

Impacting their own well-being builds trust

A horse can impact his own well-being, when he's allowed to express himself and walk away without any adverse consequence. This is a major way to build trust, especially with a horse that has had negative experiences with humans. Tension comes when a horse is "not allowed" or told "this is wrong." When everything he does is okay, even walking away, he can relax!

It shows I'm listening

I can easily approach my horse from different angles or make the distance bigger when we play at liberty. When I see him raise his head or show any other signs that my approach is a possible threat, I walk away and increase the distance. This tells my horse I'm listening. The next time, I'll try approaching from a different side and see if my horse responds differently.

It's easy

It's easy to focus on myself and self-regulate, because I don't have a horse attached to me. I can focus on becoming the human my horse wants to be with. Also, there are no reins to interfere or to nibble on, and no leadrope to get tangled up in.

All these steps give my horse a sense of control, which improves his sense of well-being. Giving my horse control is empowering him. When I have him on a lead, they're often trained to accept. Training becomes so much easier, more fun, and more beautiful when you wait for your horse to be ready to interact with you.

Liberty will show the difference between an obedient or "well-educated" horse versus a horse who willingly cooperates in a partnership based on trust. That's why these initial liberty sessions are so powerful.

As you work toward becoming the human your horse wants to be with, start with the exercises for self-regulation from Part III. Here are a few additional tips you can try:

Mirror your horse

Walk with your horse and match his steps. Look in the same direction your horse is looking. Wait when he stops. Synchronize your movement with your horse. If he walks away, that's okay. You're giving him a choice. Just catch up again later.

Mutual grooming

Horses don't groom with every horse; they have selected friends they groom with. Find the favorite spot of your horse, whether it's the wither, neck or belly. Let your horse know that it is okay to groom you back. I offer my shoulder or my back, making sure I wear a coat that can handle a bit of teeth scratching.

Compassionate curiosity

Don't get emotional! Often I see people get frustrated or angry when their horse doesn't do the thing they want him to do, or the horse walks away. Try to practice *compassionate curiosity* instead. Say, "Hmm, that's interesting; why does my horse do this?" Be curious and experiment. "What will happen if I do this? What if I change my position?"

Ask questions and say thank you!

Instead of giving your horse "what to do" commands, ask questions. When your horse gives an answer, you have a reason to say "thank you." I ask questions and I accept "no" for an answer. When my horse responds in a positive way, I say "thank you." For instance I ask, "Can we go?" together with my breathing and energy gestures. When my horse starts moving, I express gratitude for his cooperation by saying "thank you." This inviting energy not only builds trust, but also puts me in a state of heart coherence, a state where I'm calm, present and focused, which horses naturally gravitate towards.

Allow them to eat

If there isn't an arena available, you can also do this liberty session in the pasture. I do the same steps as mentioned above and allow my horses to eat if they want to, reinforcing the idea they can influence their own well-being during our sessions.

Work with two (or more) horses

When my horses are in the field together, I love to play with them there at liberty. First I go into the field to say hi and connect with them. I may sit in their presence for a while. Then I'll go to one horse and invite him to walk with me. I bring energy into my body and then bring my hand and energy forward. I may play a bit on a circle and then breathe out, stop and let him graze again. This session will only take one to two minutes. Then I go to my other horse and do the same. This automatically gives the first one a break and, if he enjoyed the bit of exercise we did, he will join me for the next session when it's his turn. This makes it fun, playful and educational for all of us!

As you do your liberty session, you might notice your horses showing signs of relaxation such as snorting, lowering their head, or having floppy ears. These are all good signs that they're becoming more comfortable with you.

It's all about building *trust*. That's why it's important to check in with yourself regularly too. Are you relaxed? Is there any tension in your body? Your horse will pick up on your energy, so the more relaxed and grounded you are, the safer your horse feels.

The end goal of this kind of liberty session is to create a safe space for your horse—a bubble where he feels comfortable and secure. When you achieve this, your horse will start seeking your company not because he has to, but because he wants to. That's when you know you've built a trusting relationship with your horse.

I also use these kinds of liberty sessions when my horse is ready for a new step in our training. For example, my first time introducing the saddle, I started with a saddle pad and did similar approach-and-retreat sessions with the pad in my hands. Again, my horse was free to walk away and give me a "no" without any consequence. I would let him investigate the pad, take it in his mouth, even stamp on it. Then I asked, "Can I rub you?" or "Can I put the pad on your back?" I said "thank you" when he allowed me, and walked away when I saw signs of "no," telling my horse I noticed his tension and that I was listening.

If I was to use a leadrope, I'd probably be able to get him to stand still and allow me to put the pad on him; however, in doing so, I don't know if he's just complying or if he stands still through voluntary cooperation and understanding. I want to ask his permission and I want him to be 100 percent okay with me putting anything on his back. I want him to trust me, knowing I'll never do anything he's afraid of or not ready for.

However, liberty training isn't about letting your horse do whatever he wants. It's important you stay safe and that your horse doesn't run you over. In the next chapter I'll talk about this and other kinds of boundaries.

Note: A short video I once posted on Instagram (less than sixty seconds), playing at liberty with my horse Jajão and me self-regulating during a short pause, went viral and gained a million views within two weeks. To remind you, you can find the link to that video at the beginning of this book.

CHAPTER 40

Setting Boundaries

The idea of giving horses a choice or an option to say "no" may raise questions about safety, especially when working at liberty or dealing with a pushy horse. I believe horses, like children, need boundaries to feel safe. They need a frame in which they can freely express themselves. That's why I want them to respect my personal space, not only for safety reasons (although maintaining your own safety is of course very important too). I call it "clarity with softness."

When working at liberty, your safety should be your number-one priority. *You* need to feel safe first, in order to hold space for your horse to feel safe. This is how I do it: I visualize my personal space, creating a strong energy bubble around me. My own horses are allowed to come very close, as I know them very well. With horses I don't know, I'm very clear about my personal space.

I always bring a "space protector," a leadrope or a whip, when I first meet a horse I don't know. If the horse comes too close to me, I first gently ask him to step back by making myself bigger and taking one step in his direction. If he doesn't respond to this, I use my space protector. I either swing the lead rope around my waist or gently swing the whip in front of me, without looking at the horse. By doing this, I'm saying, "Wait a minute, you came too

167

close. This is my personal space, and I'm protecting it." Neither tool is *ever* directed at the horse to chase him away. I use the space protector simply to claim my personal space.

While setting your boundaries, it's important to remain calm and composed. There should be no emotion involved, only a gentle request for the horse to move out of your space. The goal is not to scare the horse away but to communicate your boundary.

There are times when I don't give my horse any other choice than to listen to me; for instance, when their or my safety is at risk, or when crossing a road. While liberty sessions allow us to give horses the freedom to make choices, there are also instances when this freedom must be limited for the sake of the horse's safety, for instance when they panic and want to jump over a fence.

The key takeaway here is: safety first. You, your horse and the environment, including the people around you, need to be safe.

CHAPTER 41

Fun! Introducing Play and Enticing Curiosity

Horses often become curious when they encounter something new or different. Because horses are naturally prey animals, they're always observant of their surroundings, even when they seem to be resting or focused on eating. They may become aware of a person or object using their hearing or sense of smell long before they can see the new situation.

Horses have a powerful sense of smell, which is often overlooked. When horses smell something interesting, you might see their nostrils flaring as they gather more information using their sensitive nose. Then they touch the object with their sensitive vibrissae, also known as "whiskers." These vibrissae grow around the muzzle, nostrils, lips and eyes. The roots of the vibrissae are embedded in the deep layers of dermis and include nerve endings, so they're a protective, sensory organ of the horse and should therefore never be cut!

Introducing play and enticing curiosity is another way to help your horse feel good and move through the different states of the nervous system. Always give your horse the choice to participate in suggested play; never force play upon your horse. Entice his natural exploration behavior with new toys, food puzzles, your own expressive behavior, and introducing him to new objects during a walk in nature. It's important to enrich his environment for mental stimulation and to relieve boredom.

Wild horses move through different terrain, encountering rivers, trees, other animals and additional stimuli all the time. Our domestic horses often have limited turnout and need variation and mental stimulation in their life. Encouraging curiosity can make your horse more confident and comfortable in new environments, which helps immensely when you want to take your horse out for a relaxed trail ride.

When you play with your horse on a regular basis, and it makes him feel good, the anticipation will release dopamine, which is the "feel good" hormone. Let him explore new objects and environments at his own pace, preferably at liberty and without a halter. Wearing a halter usually signals to the horse that he needs to go somewhere or it's time to work. Many horses may expect to be corrected or even punished if they try to explore and investigate.

Make sure he has a choice to not engage, so the intrinsic seeking reflexes are activated, and not the sympathetic part of the nervous system. Dopamine is activated by the seeking system. Seeking is all about expectation. Stay under his threshold and make it fun. Play benefits a good relationship. It promotes social bonding. It helps your horse become braver and more accepting of new situations. Enrichment that encourages investigation is a win for both you and your horse!

Let's look again at the "loading a horse in a trailer" example from Chapter 17. What if you could make a mindset shift and change the trailer-loading session into an observation training for you? You could try to observe the first signal that your horse is approaching a threshold, and then take your horse away from the trailer to self-regulate and consolidate the information thus far learned while still feeling safe. Help your horse increase his Window of Tolerance and become more confident by inviting him to stamp on the ramp and explore the trailer from all sides.

Play can also positively influence the outcome of your training, as it makes the training more fun, inducing a positive, emotional state.

There was a time that I was focused on teaching my other horse Seni the piaffe. I was told to hold him in front and tap from behind, so the energy would go up. When I would take off the bridle, however, Seni would look away. I felt devastated, as it felt like I was gaining muscles but losing the heart of my horse.

I didn't do anything with him for a few months, telling him I was sorry and focusing only on regaining his trust and connecting deeply with him again. We both loved this undemanding time together; however, now his muscles started to disappear.

I wanted to train him again, but only from a place of honest communication and true connection. I introduced play and liberty. I focused on breathing, my body language, energy, and the subtle signals he was giving me. I found my "middle" between connection and physical training; or in other words, I did physical training from a place of connection. I don't need to ride in competitions and have a judge tell me how "good" I am; I want my horse to be my teacher and my number-one fan.

So don't get too serious in your training. Find your own "middle" and make it *fun* for both of you!

CHAPTER 42

Soft Touch

On my journey to better understand and connect with my horses, I found an incredibly powerful tool—soft touch. This technique was introduced to me when I started to study the Masterson Method in 2012. The Masterson Method is a technique of soft touch and gentle movement in a relaxed state to help the horse release physical and mental tension.

I was amazed by the releases that horses offered after the softest touch, sometimes not even touching the horse (called "air-gap"). When I asked why this was so effective, Jim Masterson, founder of the Masterson Method, answered, "Because we're working on the nervous system." That's when I became fascinated with the working of the nervous system.

Soft touch is a powerful co-regulating tool. It's as if we're speaking directly to their nervous system, creating a language transcending words. The power of soft touch is that you're staying under the brace of the horse so the horse doesn't feel the need to engage in a defense mechanism. This is sending a signal to the brain that it's safe (via the sensory nerves), which makes the brain send a signal back to the area where your hand is to relax (via the motor nerves).

Here are three powerful co-regulating techniques with soft touch:

Soft touch and breathing

Just as full, deep breathing is important for our own self-regulation, the same applies to horses. They too can hold their breath or breathe shallowly. By combining the power of soft touch with an invitation for deeper breathing, we can help them expand their ribcage and breathe more fully. When you put your hands gently on the ribs, you invite your horse to breathe more deeply, which helps him relax and shift into the parasympathetic nervous system.

Before you begin, take a moment to do a quick self-check and regulate yourself. Take a deep breath, feel your feet, do a little shake, and make sure your neck and shoulders are loose and relaxed. Then, place your hands softly on your horse's ribcage. Feel his breath—in and out, in and out. Move your hands gently with the rhythm of your horse's breath. Then consciously slow down your own breathing and invite your horse to do the same. It's like slowing down your hand movement, inviting him to move his breathing in sync and expand his ribcage.

This exercise isn't just about touch; it's about communication. Through the soft pressure of your hands on the ribcage, you're sending signals to your horse's brain that he's safe. In response, his brain communicates back to the body, signaling it's okay to relax. It's a beautiful conversation happening right beneath your fingertips.

Watch for signs that your horse is shifting into the parasympathetic nervous system—a deep sigh, licking and chewing, or lowering their head. These are all indicators he's relaxing and releasing tension. It's an incredible experience, standing there with your horse, your nervous systems communicating in harmony.

Hand on heart

Another technique is holding your horse's heart between your hands. This might sound poetic, but it's grounded in the practical understanding of how horses respond to our touch and energy. It involves placing one hand on your horse's chest, right where his heart beats, and the other on the withers. In this way, you're metaphorically holding his heart between your hands.

Before starting, remember that your own state and frame of mind need to be regulated and calm. Feel your feet firmly planted on the ground. Then visualize a beam of light, warmth or comfort flowing from one hand to the other, enveloping your horse's heart. This visualization can be powerful. Sometimes, you might even feel a tingle between your hands.

When your horse is still restless and wants to move, don't give up. Breathe and radiate that you are there to help him. Walk with your horse if he needs to move. Let him know you are there with him, seeing what he sees, tuning into what he experiences.

Use your energy to communicate that it's okay to relax, to let go of the alertness.

As you do this, watch for signs of relaxation in your horse. He might start licking and chewing, his head might lower, his eyes might soften. These are all indications that he's shifting into the parasympathetic nervous system, their "rest and digest" state.

One key thing to remember during this process is to throw away the clock. This isn't about achieving a result in a defined timeframe. Instead, it's about being fully present with your horse, allowing him to relax at his own pace.

This method of co-regulation can be powerful. It's not just about the physical touch; it's about holding space for your horse, providing comfort and safety, inviting him to be with you in a state of relaxation. It's about holding his heart between your hands and communicating your care and connection.

Release tension in the TMJ

Another great way to help your horse is releasing tension in the temporomandibular joint. This small joint stores a lot of tension, for both horses and humans. The jaw is a hub of tension for many horses; not just those who've experienced the pull of a bit or halter, but all horses. Clenching teeth is a natural reaction to stressful situations. It's almost magical what happens when you put your fingers gently on the joint, or cover it very softly with your whole hand.

To practice this technique, first ensure you're in a relaxed state. Remember, your energy greatly influences your horse's emotional state. Place two fingers gently on your horse's TMJ, located in a little vertical groove behind the cheekbone. If you can't locate the groove, simply rest your whole hand on the area where you feel the little bump.

Your horse might fidget, trying to move away. Don't be disheartened. This fidgeting often precedes a release. Keep your hand softly placed on the TMJ, breathe deeply, and wait. Remember, patience is key.

If your horse still seems unable to release the tension, sometimes stepping away can help. Some horses need a little space to let go. As you step back, do your own jaw release. You will often see them start to lick and chew, lower their head or even yawn once you step away.

The TMJ is connected to the hyoid bone, which in turn connects to the front legs and runs through the fascia lines of the entire body of your horse. By releasing tension in the TMJ, you help him relax throughout his whole body. This technique is a gentle invitation for your horse to let go of stored tension. It's about communicating your care and understanding, showing him that it's safe to relax with you.

CHAPTER 43

Expand to Build Resilience

This last chapter is about expanding and exploring to build resilience. Similar to what we explained in Part III about what you can do for yourself to increase your resilience, you can also help your horse to become more resilient. You can help your horse widen the Window of Tolerance, so it becomes easier for him to cope with new or unexpected situations.

This doesn't mean overwhelming him with constant new experiences. It's about asking a little bit more, then returning to a familiar, safe space. It's about exploring new situations while you're there, being his safe spot, radiating calmness and assurance.

Now, what if your horse says no? This can basically mean two things:

1. *"I don't feel safe!"*
2. *"I don't understand, I'm confused, but I still feel safe!"*

In the first option, this "no" can manifest as either a fight-or-flight response (i.e. the sympathetic state) or a complete withdrawal from the situation (i.e. the dorsal vagal state's red zone).

In such instances, it's vital to respect your horse's "no." A horse that doesn't feel at ease is not in a learning state of mind. Your primary task becomes helping him feel safe again, guiding him back into a receptive learning state.

With the second option, if the "no" stems from confusion or unfamiliarity but the horse still feels safe, it's okay to ask again or ask in a different way. Gently encourage your horse to step out of his comfort zone, then guide him back into the green zone again afterwards.

This is where the concept of building resilience comes in. Increasing resilience involves introducing your horse to new situations like exposing him to different animals, or bringing him to a new location. It's about helping him cope with different situations, to increase his comfort zone gradually.

When you're training your horse, he might also give you a "no." You can respond similarly, based on where the "no" stems from. Applying the polyvagal principles to horse training doesn't mean your horse needs to be relaxed all the time. It's about helping him move through all the states effortlessly, so he can self-regulate quickly and easily in all circumstances.

There's actually a curve that explains the relationship between arousal and performance, along with an optimal level of arousal for maximal performance, known as the **Yerkes-Dodson law**. I've added an explanation in the appendices.

These last illustrations, based on a real training session, show beautifully how Jajão is moving from an explosive state, to calm and connected and then to cool and collected, showing a moderate arousal for optimal collection!

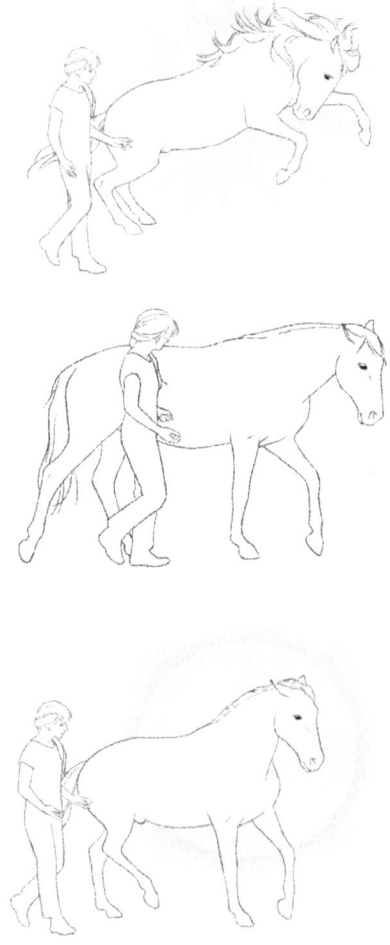

Become a nervous system navigator and help your horse to become a nervous system navigator as well. The best gift you can give your horse is to help him cope and feel safe in our human world!

APPENDICES

APPENDIX 1

Golden Rules for You

We are wired for love and connection, but we forget this when we're in survival mode. I've summarized some "golden rules" here as a quick reference, to help get out of survival mode and remember who you truly are.

Become an observer of yourself.

Check in with yourself.

Practice self-regulation on a daily basis.

Choose your favorite strategies and set your own emergency routine.

Breathe deeply.

Become heart coherent.

Shake it! Get rid of tension.

Choose your emotion.

Express gratitude and say "thank you."

Learn to switch between states and increase your resilience.

Don't be too serious; have fun!

Soften your jaw, shoulders, ribs, eyes, neck, back, arms and legs.

Ask yourself: Can I move freely and lightly?

Get to know your authentic self and be *you*. The biggest stress in life is trying to be someone you're not.

Practice self-care. You can only look after others (including your horse) if you look after yourself first.

Create a list of your favorite activities, so you have options when you want to switch to another state. When you're in a distressed state, it's hard to think of things you like. That's why it's great to have a list, so you can just pick one.

When you feel challenged, ask yourself, "What would love do?"

APPENDIX 2

Yerkes-Dodson Law: The Stress-Performance Curve

The Yerkes-Dobson law describes the relationship between increased levels of arousal and performance.

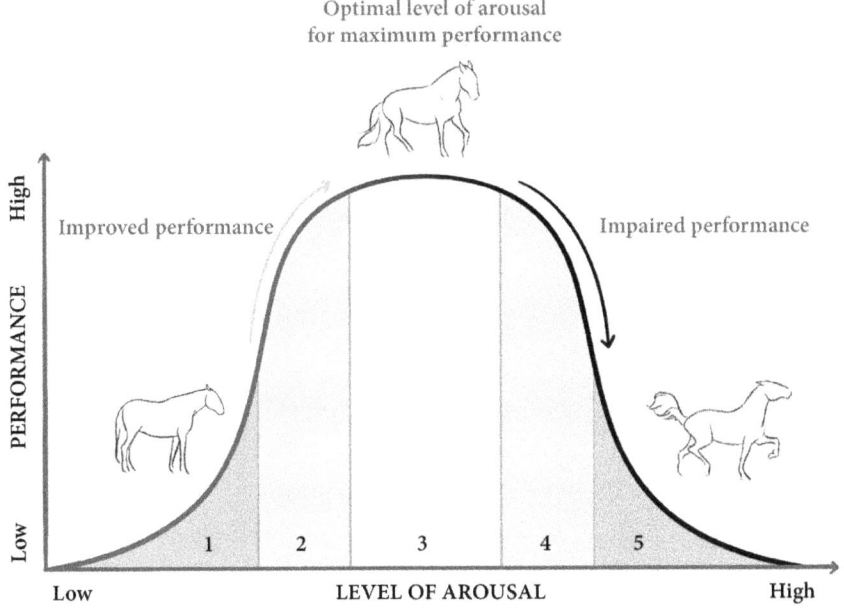

Here's a breakdown:

1. Low Arousal: When under very low levels of stress or arousal, performance is not optimal due to lack of motivation and/or too much relaxation.

2. Moderate Arousal: With a bit of arousal, performance generally improves. Here alertness, motivation and focus are increasing, leading to better performance.

3. Optimal Arousal: At the peak of the curve, peak performance is shown, with an ideal balance between alertness, arousal and motivation.

4. High Arousal: When more energy or stress is added beyond the peak performance, performance starts to decrease. This decreasing performance is due to anxiety, reduced concentration, and a decrease in fine motor skills.

5. Very High Arousal: When stress becomes extremely high, performance will drop drastically due to overwhelm, extreme stress and shutdown behavior.

The optimal level of arousal varies from person to person and from horse to horse. As we learned in this book, both you and your horse can develop skills and strategies to manage stress, become more resilient, and optimize performance.

Next Steps

Congratulations!

You've come to the end of this book, gaining a deep understanding of Polyvagal Theory and its transformative impact on horse training. With this knowledge, you're better equipped to recognize the nervous system states in your horse and build a harmonious relationship that transcends traditional training methods.

You now know how to become a nervous system navigator! By practicing self-regulation and co-regulation techniques, you'll find the way to true connection, trust, and harmonious partnership with your horse. You're now ready for a lifelong journey of joy, understanding and fulfillment in everything you do with your horse. The power of true connection lies in your hands, and your equine companion awaits your guidance and compassion.

Remember, to rewire your brain, repetition is the key! By reading this book, you've gained new understanding; however, to really become the safe spot for your horse and set up your training for success, you need to practice!

I've put together additional resources that will help you put into practice what you've learned. I mentioned it at the beginning of this book, but here's the link again:

https://rebrand.ly/W4Cbook

The content of this book is also available as an online class. If you're a visual learner and want to dive deeper into the polyvagal approach to horse training, then I warmly invite you to join my **Wired 4 Connection** course. You can find more information on my website, **lucieklaassen.com.**

ACKNOWLEDGEMENTS

First I want to say thank you to Ellen Schuthof. She called me when she was looking for someone who would be a good match for Jajão. That's how Jajão came into my life, even though I wasn't looking for another horse.

Much of the information in this book was learned through studying with and learning from Jim Masterson, Dr. Stephen Peters and therapist Sarah Schlote. I'm grateful for their work in explaining these sometimes complex subjects to the public in an understandable way. I encourage you to visit **equusoma.com**, **horsebrainscience.info** and **mastersonmethod.com** to learn about these topics in more detail.

A big thank you to Rozenn Grosjean for creating all the illustrations in this book. Working with you is always such a pleasure! Thank you also to Anne Mette Graumann for the beautiful cover image and Susan Wijs for the great author image.

I also want to thank everyone who read my book in the making, gave me tips on what to include, asked me critical questions, and gave me great feedback and encouragement. Also, special thanks to all the participants of the Wired 4 Connection online course for great questions and suggestions on what to include in the book. Special thanks to Kim Harrison, Klaske van der Horst and Hetty Koenraads who provided me with great and detailed feedback!

Richard Ricks made my brain dumps of information into readable language, and Jason Pettus did a great job editing this book. Thank you both for making this book an easy read! Karen Pina supported me in the process of writing and publishing my first book. Thank you so much for your guidance.

Lastly, I want to thank *you* for your interest in this topic, and for taking the time to read this book. Thank you for helping me create a more compassionate world for horses!

BIBLIOGRAPHY

Dr. Stephen Porges (2017). *The Pocket Guide to the Polyvagal Theory: The Transformative Power of Feeling Safe*

Deb Dana (2021). *Anchored: How to Befriend Your Nervous System*

Bessel van der Kolk (2014). *The Body Keeps the Score: Mind, Brain and Body in the Transformation of Trauma*

Peter A. Levine (1997). *Waking the Tiger*

Gabor Maté, Daniel Maté (2022). *The Myth of Normal: Trauma, Illness & Healing in a Toxic Culture*

Daniel Siegel (2011). *Mindsight: Transform Your Brain with the New Science of Kindness*

Bruce Lipton (2015). *The Biology of Belief: Unleashing the Power of Consciousness, Matter & Miracles*

Rachael Draaisma (2018). *Language Signs and Calming Signals of Horses*

Jim Masterson (2011). *Beyond Horse Massage: Introducing the Masterson Method* (also see mastersonmethod.com)

Dr. Stephen Peters, Martin Black (2021). *Evidence Based Horsemanship* (also see horsebrainscience.info)

Sarah Schlote. equusoma.com

Doc Childre et al. heartmath.org

Wim Hof. wimhofmethod.com

ABOUT THE AUTHOR

When she was a little girl, Lucie Klaassen developed a deep love for horses. They were her safe place when she was young. She spent every free minute with them and that's how she developed a very natural way of being and communicating with horses.

Lucie teaches international Balanced Rider & Horse clinics and Body Awareness for Riders workshops, including the polyvagal principles. She is also a coach in Equine Assisted Development and has been guiding hundreds of people with her online programs.

Lucie resides in the Netherlands with her two horses, Seni and Jajão. She helps passionate horse people all over the world reconnect with their body wisdom so they can connect with their horse from the heart.

Help Me Help Horses!

Thank you for reading my book!

I really appreciate your valuable feedback and
I love hearing what you have to say.

Please take a minute or two and leave your honest review here:

https://rebrand.ly/W4CBookReview

Let's make this world a more compassionate one for horses!

Thank you so much!

Lucie Klaassen